DEDICATION: To the prophet who lives in Charlotte (Eph. 5:17)

Printed by CreateSpace, An Amazon.com Company

Available on Amazon.com and other online stores

THE CALL Logo by Mary Thurman

Author's Note: Most of the stories in this book are actual, true life events. A few of the stories are allegorical, although they may be based on real events. The names of persons described have been changed to protect their privacy.

TABLE OF CONTENTS

PROLOGUE

When I was a teenager in the mid-1970's, my father gave me a 1964 Volkswagen Beetle to drive. The Volkswagen Beetle was a triumph of automotive genius. The motor was a simple and efficient machine created by a German master designer. It powered the car using four cylinders intended to fire in sequence producing a cycle that recurred over and over again. If all of the cylinders functioned well, and operated properly in relationship to each other, then the engine produced 40 horsepower which was plenty of pep for such a lightweight and aerodynamic vehicle.

If, however, any one of the cylinders was missing a key component, or if the cylinders did not work in proper order, the engine lacked power. To my chagrin, the VW that my father let me drive was in this latter category. The engine started, but when I pressed the accelerator, the car barely moved. If I floored the accelerator on level terrain, that VW would not go more than 20 miles per hour. The car barely worked.

It was humiliating. On those curvy mountain roads, there were not many places to pass. As I crept down the road with the accelerator jammed to the floor, a line of cars slowly gathered behind me, many of them operated by drivers upset at being held up by such a slow moving vehicle. When I finally reached a passing zone, other drivers honked in frustration as they passed. A few leaned out the window and yelled "Get off the road!"

Even worse, I didn't know what was wrong with the vehicle. It felt to me as if one of the cylinders didn't work. The engine sounded as if it barely completed its intended cycle. Something was wrong with it, but what? I didn't have a clue. I wasn't a mechanic, and at that tender age, I didn't know where to turn for help. That dysfunction was really all that I knew, so I continued to crawl around town without seeking assistance from a professional.

What I did know was how driving that vehicle made me feel ... BAD. It was mortifying for a teenager. I wondered if my father took some secret delight from the fact that his teenage son drove a defective vehicle absolutely incapable of going the speed limit, much less exceeding it. My friends laughed at my car. Surely this driving experience was not what those German engineers intended from their brilliant design.

Then, as I was slouched in my seat one day with my car limping along, the motor backfired loudly. KAPOW! I slumped further down certain that the dysfunctional engine had finally given up the ghost. But the next instant, the engine roared to life and zoomed with power. The car sped up to 35 miles per hour before I realized that I would lose control of the vehicle if I did not let the accelerator up off the floor! From that point on, that VW ran great and had plenty of pep.

When I got home and told my father, he just shook his head and shrugged his shoulders. My attitude about driving sure changed, though. Having an engine that operated in the way that the designer intended made all the difference in the world! No longer did I slouch in my seat and try to hide my face. I sat up and smiled as I tootled about town. I felt as if I ruled the road!

At times, my attempts at ministry felt like I was operating a dysfunctional VW Beetle. I had a ministry model that I drove, but it really didn't work well. Maybe a key part was missing. Maybe the ministry had all the parts, but they didn't work together well. Often, we don't know the cause of the problems. Strangely, though, we don't stop and take the time to find out. We just limp along because that model is all we know. We do it because we have always done it that way.

We are painfully aware that the ministry does not work well – certainly not in the way that God intended. In fact, we may even be ashamed of its pitiful output. We, however, are so accustomed to driving like a tortoise that we are not willing to make a change. If we just knew the wonderful things that God intended, and what it felt like to fulfill the potential that He put in us, we would seek help and fix it in a heartbeat!

Thankfully, God has given us a vehicle to use for ministry in His kingdom. He has designed it perfectly to operate with power and stature. Like the cycle of the engine of a car, God has created a sequential cycle of discipleship that is designed to recur over and over again. The Bible details it. It is cycle of growth, maturation, training, and reproduction ordained by God for His church. The cycle has five essential aspects that are intended to work in proper order. If all parts of this cycle are functioning properly, the Body of Christ operates with power. And it grows! If, however. any one of the five aspects is missing, or if the five do not work in proper order, then the whole cycle falters and the Body limps along.

This book is important because it describes this sequential cycle of discipleship in detail.

Before we can implement this cycle, though, we need to understand the purpose that God has for us. This book is important to YOU because this book can assist you in discovering your place in the Kingdom of God. God is calling each of us to minister within His Kingdom. God is the Source of call. When we understand the call that God has on our lives, then we can use the gifts God has given us to fulfill that call, and realize His purpose for our life and work.

For that reason, this book begins by exploring call from God – how God calls His people, and what God calls His people to do. In the first four chapters, we will review the ways God called His saints, and how God cultivated the character and attitudes in His people that enabled them to fulfill the specific destiny to which He called them.

The next five chapters describe the fulfillment of call and five areas of ministry that God gives His people so that they can accomplish His work. Each chapter details a necessary function in the sequential cycle that God has ordained. God sends a person with a word from Him to share with others, to care for others, and to teach others to walk in His ways.

The kingdom cycle is vital for us as individuals. Through participation in a functioning cycle, individuals realize their destiny in God - reaching maturity and completeness. Completeness occurs when a person fulfills the destiny that God has given him. We are created beings. God created us for His purpose to fulfill His plans. That is our destiny. As we discover His will - His purpose for our lives – and then walk in it, we realize completeness.

The last six chapters shift to a more corporate focus. The kingdom cycle is not just vital for us as individuals. The cycle is vital for us as a Body. Through God's intended cycle, the Body of Christ matures into its destiny in God - achieving completeness. These final chapters explain the cycle and how individual Christians fit into God's plan as effective and functioning members of His glorious Body. They detail how saints can function cooperatively to complete the mission that God has entrusted to His Church.

"And we proclaim Him, admonishing every man and teaching every man with all wisdom, that we may present every man complete in Christ. And for this purpose also I labor, striving according to His power, which mightily works within me." Col. 1:28-29.

SECTION ONE

PREPARATION FOR CALL

LESSON 1 - WHAT IS CALL?

I stood on a bedraggled, postage stamp field with a whistle in my mouth. I was surrounded by young men kicking up a cloud of dust by playing with a soccer ball. It was weekly soccer on Sunday just like any other Sunday. As I contemplated my surroundings, it felt almost surreal.

The young men were ages eight to eighteen. I was the only person over twenty. In fact, I was at least twenty years older than any other person there.

Not only was I older, but I was also different culturally than anyone else. Most of these young men were international refugees from countries ravaged by civil war or political turmoil. There were players from Vietnam, Bosnia, Somalia, Honduras and Liberia. There were blacks, Asians, Hispanics, Arabs, and Slavs. I was the lone American.

And the language. I was the only person for whom English was a native tongue. Some of the young men had recently arrived in America and spoke almost no English. We communicated by gestures and facial expressions. Other young men could speak a little English. But when I asked them to interpret for the non-English speakers, I could never be sure I was getting an accurate retelling. Based on the laughter and coy looks that occurred between languages, I often doubted the trustworthiness of the translation.

As I considered the scene, it seemed as if the boys and I had nothing in common. I asked myself, "What are you doing out here?"

"What are you doing out here?" This question rang through my mind as the afternoon progressed. "Progressed" is probably a euphemistic word. On this day, I had thirty energetic young men buzzing around a field that could realistically accommodate a maximum of twelve players at one time. I tried to rotate teams and players. At times I felt as if we had a soccer game on the field and a three-ring circus off of it.

Dysfunctions were on ample display. On the sidelines, bikes whizzed, balls bounced, and fists flew. Fighting is a part of some cultural lifestyles. Abu from Somalia and Baker from Bosnia were playing in the soccer game on the field on opposite teams. During the match, they started taunting each other. I stopped the game to warn them and to encourage them to calm down.

When we restarted the game, though, they began fouling each other - the type of foul that occurs when the ball is in the vicinity, but the obvious target of the kick is the other person's legs. I again paused the game to give them an opportunity to cool off, but I felt helpless. I knew what was coming, but there really wasn't much I could do to stop it.

Mercifully, Abu's team scored and that game ended. But as Abu and Baker passed each other leaving the field, Abu sneered and taunted Baker. It was like lighting a match. Abu and Baker immediately dove into each other with fists flying. It wasn't a restrained bout. They both lost complete control and threw windmill haymakers with intent to injure.

Wading into the middle of this type of fight could be a dangerous venture. Because of my experience, I usually gave the combatants a few seconds to expend a little energy and to release their most violent frustrations before interceding - hoping, of course, that no one would suffer serious bodily harm in the interim. After a flurry of punches, I stepped in to separate them. I bearhugged Baker, while a couple of Abu's friends pulled him away still struggling to get at Baker. When a semblance of order was restored, Abu was bent at the waist. One friend held his left arm with both hands, and another had his right arm in a half nelson, with the forearm behind Abu's neck, holding him down.

From his bent stance, Abu looked up at Baker, and held out his arm to offer his hand to him. "Good fight," he said.

"Good fight!" I shook my head and blinked in disbelief. I thought, "A minute ago you would have killed him if you had the means, and now you say 'Good fight'?!?!

"What-" I asked myself, "what are you doing out here?"

"And where is everybody?" I looked over the field. I stood out like a sore thumb. "Here I am out on this field week after week, year after year, alone. Where are the people from my church? No one else seems to share this vision."

Discouraged, I stopped the games for the afternoon, sent the guys home, and piled the soccer gear into my car. On the drive home, I hung my head in despair, close to tears. This outreach was not going as planned.

That evening and over the next week, I did some soul searching. If I was doing any good out on that field, I really couldn't tell it. We couldn't even get through an afternoon of soccer

8

without a brawl, much less impact lives. Were my efforts futile?

No one wanted to do what I did. If this outreach had a vision, that vision hadn't inspired anyone else to partner in the ministry. At times, it seemed like madness - to do the same thing week after week with the same results.

As I reviewed the situation, I didn't have much to hang my hat on. Why should I continue the work? I had only one reason left. One thread held me in. It was the knowledge of a memory. I knew that at one point that God, through a series of events and through what I thought was inspiration, had called me to do what I was doing. He had called me to use soccer as a means to impact the lives of young men. At that point, the memory of that call was all that I had to keep me going.

But that call was real to me, and I had resolved to obey it. Despite my angst, I decided that my duty was to obey. God would determine the results.

On the next Sunday at 2:30 PM, I was back at the same field, feeling alone, surrounded by foreign young men.

THE MEANING OF CALL

I was young, but I was intent on hearing from God. I went to a mall in Alabama and sat on a bench in the walkway. Person after person meandered by me. I was waiting - waiting and listening. I sat there for what seemed a long time.

A bookstore caught my eye. Unsure of its significance, I got up and went inside of it. While walking through the bookstore, I was struck by a contrast. On one wall were "inspirational" books - Bibles, concordances, dictionaries, devotionals, meditations and Christian biographies. Immediately across from the inspirational section was a section of obscure craft - astrology, magic, tarot cards, witchcraft, and other black arts. From a commercial perspective, the placement made sense. Both sections concerned spiritualism. From a Christian perspective, it was a contradiction. Darkness adjoined light. The "dark" wall left me with a sense of foreboding.

As I stood there trying to discern, four people walked up - a young man, a young

woman (apparently the young man's wife or girlfriend), and two elderly ladies. By his words and actions, the young man was leading the expedition. Walking over to the "dark" section, he said, "Let's buy a book on astrology. I like those."

One of the elderly ladies seemed leery. "I don't know," she said hesitantly. It occurred to me that she was probably financing the purchase.

The young lady chimed in, "Horoscopes are fun, and they tell you a lot about your future. Let's find one."

"Yes," said the man decisively. "We are going to get one of these books." He began to peruse the astrological selection.

I only had a New Testament with me, so I picked up a Bible from the inspirational section. Walking over to the group, I asked, "Pardon me. Do you mind if I read something to you from the Bible?"

No one answered. They were a little taken aback. I didn't give them a further chance to respond and began reading from Isaiah 47:

"You who are wearied with your many counsels;

Let now the astrologers,

Those who prophesy by the stars,

Those who predict by the new moons,

Stand up and save you from what will come upon you.

Behold, they have become like stubble,

Fire burns them;

They can not deliver themselves from the power of the flame..." (Isa. 47:13-15)

I closed the Bible and looked at the group. Immediately, it was as if roles had changed and authority had passed. The older lady, who had been following the young man through the store, took charge.

"Come on," she said firmly. "We aren't going to buy any of those books. They aren't good. Let's go."

The young man put the astrology book back on the shelf. Without a word, he and the young lady meekly followed the two older ladies out of the bookstore.

I put the Bible back on the shelf, feeling that I had been led to the right place at the

right time with the right words. As I left the bookstore, the irony struck me. I had used the store's own book to stop a purchase from it.

Call is simply a leading or direction from the Lord intended for one or more persons. Through the Holy Spirit, the voice of the Lord expresses His will. It is an invitation to obedience.

Call can be short or it can be long. A call can last for a few moments; or for a season; or it can endure a lifetime.

Call can be one small action; or a series of actions; or it can be a thousand crusades.

Call can impact one person; or a few people; or it can impact a city or even nations. Or call can be to a method or to a certain type of ministry.

Call can direct a person to do the same thing every time, or use a different approach in each different situation.

Call is a vision pulling the saint in one direction rather than the other. "When he [Paul] had seen the vision, immediately we sought to go into Macedonia, concluding that God *had called us* to preach the gospel to them." Acts 16:10.

Call is a dramatic epiphany that endures a lifetime. Paul, then known as Saul, experienced a call in a flash of light from heaven on the road to Damascus. Acts 9. Through this call, he received direction for the rest of his life:

And I said, "Who are you, Lord?"

And the Lord said, "I am Jesus whom you are persecuting. But get up and stand on your feet; *for this purpose* I have appeared to you, to appoint you a minister and a witness not only to the things which you have seen, but also to the things in which I will appear to you; rescuing you from the Jewish people and from the Gentiles, to whom I am sending you, to open their eyes so that they may turn from darkness to light and from the dominion of Satan to God, that they may receive forgiveness of sins and an inheritance among those who have been sanctified by faith in Me." Acts 26:15-18.

Or call is a directive to brief ministry. Immediately after his dramatic conversion, Paul's life was irrevocably impacted through a short term call to Ananias, a disciple in Damascus.

"Brother Saul, the Lord Jesus, who appeared to you on the road by which you were coming, *has sent me* so that you may regain your sight, and be filled with the Holy Spirit." Acts 9:17.

In that mall in Alabama, I experienced call for that moment. I can only describe it as a nudge or a tug. I felt a leading. If I had not responded quickly, those four people could have come and gone without hearing a timely word.

PRINCIPLE: Through call, we fulfill the plan which God holds for our life.

WHAT IS THE IMPACT OF CALL?

Here is the ministry tally:

1. Number of whippings with lashes (39 times each): 5

2. Number of times beaten with rods: 3

3. Number of stonings (left for dead): 1

4. Number of shipwrecks: 3

5. Number of hours floating in the open sea: 24

6. Without food, hungry and thirsty: Often

7. Sleepless nights: Many

8. Cold and exposed to the elements: Frequent

9. Imprisonments: Multiple

10. Other dangers experienced in travels: Flooded rivers, robbers, wild animals, and false brethren

Do you want this ministry?

This list is the ministry summary of one man - Paul. II Cor. 11:23-28. Paul continuously experienced the response of a perverse and deceived world to clear and unequivocal proclamation of Jesus Christ. He bore the brutal reaction of carnal antagonism toward the gospel.

Why did Paul keep striving in the face of such adversity? What drove him to persevere in the self-described "labor and hardship" of his ministry? I Thes. 2:9.

Paul was a man who knew he had been called by God. "But when He who had set me apart, even from my mother's womb, and *called me* through His grace, was pleased to reveal his Son in me, that I might preach Him among the Gentiles..." Gal. 1:15-16. Because his call came from God, Paul determined to obey that call regardless of resistance from man or beast.

What is the impact of call?

1.   AGENCY - When a disciple is called, he has a sense of agency - that God has authorized him to act in the realm of his calling. The disciple is not just functioning within his own program, but is representing God to those persons to whom he is called. From the beginning, Paul knew that God called him to act on His behalf. "Go, for he [Paul] is *a chosen instrument of mine*, to bear My name before the Gentiles and kings and the sons of Israel; for I will show him how much he must suffer for My name's sake." Acts 9:15-16.

Paul conveyed this feeling of agency. "We are ambassadors for Christ..." II Cor. 5:20. Because of this agency, a called disciple knows that God has empowered him to fulfill his call. "Paul, an apostle (not sent men, nor through the agency of man, but through Jesus Christ, and God the Father, who raised Him from the dead)..." Gal. 1:1. Because he has been sent by God, God stands with him in the work that he is doing.

PRINCIPLE: A called disciple is an empowered disciple.

---

2.   DIRECTION - A called disciple has a sense of direction. God has revealed His purpose for that disciple's life, so that disciple walks in it. Paul was a man of purpose. Paul was a man of purpose because he was called. Paul knew his direction early in his Christian walk.

And it came about when I returned to Jerusalem and was praying in the temple that I fell into a trance, and I saw Him saying to me, "Make haste, and get out of Jerusalem quickly, because they will not accept your testimony about Me."

13

And I said, "Lord, they themselves understand that in one synagogue after another I used to imprison and beat those who believed in Thee. And when the blood of Thy witness Stephen was being shed, I also was standing by approving, and watching out for the cloaks of those who were slaying him."

And He said to me, "Go! For I will send you far away to the Gentiles." Acts 22:17-21.

God's direction is necessary for effectiveness. Without God's guiding hand, the disciple's work will be in vain. "Unless the Lord builds a house, they labor in vain who build it; Unless the Lord guards the city, the watchman keeps awake in vain." Ps. 127:1.

PRINCIPLE: A called disciple has a sense of purpose and direction.

---

3.   PEACE - God's direction vests an assurance in ministry. The called disciple knows that he is working in accordance with God's will for his life. Peace and joy cover the disciple even in the midst of turbulent circumstances. This disciple truly realizes the meaning of Zech. 4:6 - "'Not by might, not by power, but by My Spirit' says the Lord."

A call fulfilled yields peace and joy. "I am filled with comfort; I am overflowing with joy in all our affliction." II Cor. 7:4. The place of deepest contentment for the disciple lies in the center of God's will for his life.

4.   IDENTITY - A called disciple knows he is supposed to work where he is called. His call becomes a part of him to the point that it is his identity. A called disciple can be no other.

Paul labels himself as an apostle in the first verse of nine (9) of his epistles! "Paul, a bond-servant of Christ Jesus, *called as an apostle*, set apart for the gospel of God..." Rom. 1:1. Because of his call, Paul understood the role and mission of his life. Paul knew that he was an apostle - not because he earned it, but because God called him as one. And because he obeyed.

"For I am the least of the apostles, who am not fit to be called an apostle, because I persecuted the church of God. But by the grace of God, *I am what I am*." I Cor. 15:9-10.

> PRINCIPLE: A called disciple knows who he is in the Lord.

COMMITTED

A called disciple is committed in time, in location, and in lifestyle. He will hang in a ministry long after other disciples have given up and gone home. A called disciple is like the proverbial bulldog that grabs hold and will not let go because he is obedient to his Master. I can not tell you how many times through the years I stood out on that soccer field alone wondering what in the world I was doing out there...wondering why nobody was out there with me...wondering if I was just a fool.

My discouragement on the soccer field did not wane. I always tried to share with the diverse group of guys. Because grace and the idea of forgiveness distinguish the gospel from other religions, they were often a focal point of my talks. Most times the young men were restless and disruptive when I spoke. They just wanted to play soccer. I did not know whether they understood a thing about the gospel or its message of forgiveness.

Then, one Sunday, Mahir went off on me. Mahir had a tough combination. Mahir was sensitive, but he was also insufferably stubborn. Because he was sensitive, Mahir lost his temper easily. Because he was stubborn, Mahir's tantrums were memorable.

Like many of the refugees, Mahir did not have a father in the home, and he struggled with authority. Mahir didn't like some referee calls that I made during the game that Sunday. Before long, he was cursing me up one side and down the other. He displayed as much contempt for me as he could, demonstrating that contempt with numerous obscene gestures. Seeing that didn't get a rise out of me, he began demeaning my mother and disparaging my ancestry. He concluded by questioning my manhood.

I sent the guys, including Mahir, home. I told Mahir that he was suspended from playing until further notice.

Once again, my drive home was full of despair. That evening and the next, I

mentally listed the positive and negative aspects of the outreach - the successes and the failures. My emotions went up and down as I explored the question of whether I should continue doing soccer. It was a tough issue. Finally, it still fundamentally came down to one question: "Was I called to do it?" As I carefully considered what the Lord had done in my life, I had to answer the question affirmatively. So, on the next Sunday, I was back on the soccer field, surrounded by young men.

Mahir was absent that day. During a break, another player asked, "Coach, when will Mahir be allowed to come back?"

"What can Mahir do to make it right?" I replied. "He has insulted and offended me publicly. He can't put his words back into his mouth. There is nothing that Mahir can do for me to make up for what he did."

The boys were silent. Then Isak spoke up. He was the best friend of Mahir's older brother. "Coach," he said, "Coach, you can forgive him."

I looked at Isak. I almost cried, but I probably was too stunned to do so. These young men had heard what I was sharing! I gathered myself to respond. "Yes, Isak, I can forgive him. It is the same way with us and God. We sin against Him and offend Him. But there is nothing that we can do to make it right. What can we do for God? He has everything already and He is everything.

"But" I continued, "God can forgive us. And He offers forgiveness to us just like I can choose to forgive Mahir."

My ride home from soccer that day was much more joyful than the previous week.

MEDITATION: "And we know that God causes all things to work together for good to those who love God, to those who are called according to His purpose." Rom. 8:28.

1. Have you ever experienced a call or direction from God in your life?

2. If so, what was the impact of that call on you?

3. Are there any areas of ministry to which you feel drawn?

4. What has God shown you about those areas of ministry?

5. What has happened in your life that has prepared you for those areas of ministry?

REVIEW: (Note: After each chapter, there is a review of the principles expressed in that chapter. Please take time to review those principles, and to consider how they might apply to your life, and to the lives of the believers around you.)

1. Call is a leading or direction from the Lord intended for one or more persons.
2. Through call, we fulfill the plan which God holds for our life, and we can accomplish His work.
3. A called disciple is an empowered disciple (Agency).
4. A called disciple has a sense of purpose. (Direction).
5. A called disciple can be no other (Identity).
6. A called disciple is committed in time, location and lifestyle.

REVELATION: AUTHORITY

WHOSE...   ...LORDSHIP?

LESSON 2 - THE SOURCE OF CALL

Barney was a close friend of mine. One day over lunch we explored the question, "How does a person find purpose and direction for his or her life?"

Barney said "There are so many important things in scripture. We could spend days just making lists of things we should do. Is one thing really more important than another?"

"Well," I asked, "for starters, what direction do you think Jesus gave to His disciples when He departed?"

"I don't know." Barney answered. "I guess the Great Commission?"

"I can't disagree with you there. What is the Great Commission?"

"You know. 'Go and make disciples of all nations, baptizing them in the name of the Father and the Son and the Holy Spirit, teaching them to observe all that I commanded you for I am with you always, even unto the end of the age.'" (Mt. 28:19-20)

"That's good!" I said. "But you left out an important part."

"What part?" Barney asked.

"The beginning...the foundation."

"What do you mean?"

"Jesus didn't merely say 'Go and make disciples'. He said, 'Go therefore and make disciples...' The word 'therefore' is important. It means that there is a prior premise. Jesus used the word 'therefore' because He had just given the disciples the basis for the Commission. Jesus said, 'All authority has been given to Me in heaven and on earth. Go therefore and make disciples of all nations...'" (Mt. 28:18-19a)

I paused for a moment. "We can't fulfill a call until we know the authority that commissions it."

Call and authority - the two are inextricably linked. Call and authority are inseparably

18

intertwined. As one reads the Book of Acts, one begins to realize that the Book of Acts is the story of how the disciples fulfilled Jesus' Commission. It is the story of how Jesus' disciples acted as Jesus' witnesses in Jerusalem; then in Judea, then in Samaria; then to the remotest part of the earth. Acts 1:8.

But the disciples were able to fulfill the Great Commission only because they understood the authority which they had been given. It was an authority greater than sickness (Acts 3); greater than beatings (Acts 16); greater than imprisonments (Acts 12); and even greater than death (Acts 7).

Peter and John understood the authority with which they ministered. They were commanded by the highest Jewish tribunal, the Sanhedrin, "not to speak or teach at all in the name of Jesus." Acts 4:18. This Council, led by the high priest, was the highest religious authority known to them. Peter and John had to decide whether the authority of the most revered assembly on earth was greater than the authority of their call. But Peter and John had been with Jesus and had witnessed His authority. Then Jesus expressly gave that same authority to them. So Peter and John responded: "Whether it is right in the sight of God to give heed to you rather than to God, you be the judge; for we cannot stop speaking what we have seen and heard." Acts 4:19-20. The disciples understood the authority by which they acted.

PRINCIPLE: To fulfill his call, the disciple must understand the authority of God.

WHAT IS AUTHORITY?

Authority is the power to govern, supervise or judge a person, place or thing. God possesses all authority on heaven and on earth ("absolute authority"). In accordance with His will, He shares His authority with men ("delegated authority") - which is why we should have an attitude of submission to all authority in heaven and on earth.

Paul wrote "Let every man be in subjection to the governing authorities. For there is no authority except from God, and those which exist are established by God." Rom. 13:1. Paul wrote these words to the Romans, who at that time, were subjected to torture and persecution at the hands of their government. (As an aside, note there is a difference between our response to absolute authority and to delegated authority. The response to the absolute authority of God is *complete obedience*. The response to delegated authority is an *attitude of submission* by which we have a desire to obey that authority if at all possible. I Pet. 2:13-20.)

When God issues a call, He is giving His servant(s) the authority to accomplish His work. He is not going to call a servant to a task without giving that servant the authority to fulfill it.

PRINCIPLE: A call from God is a grant of His authority.

THE FOUNDATION OF CALL

I was good friends with a local judge. He was a fine man and an upstanding judge. Billy Graham came to town and the judge went to the crusade. During the crusade, the Holy Spirit touched him. He sensed the presence of the Lord in a real and tangible way.

A few days later, I received a call from the judge. "David" he said, "I was really impacted at the Billy Graham crusade. He touched my heart. I think that the Lord is leading me to start a Bible study for local lawyers and judges. Do you think that you would like to come?"

I answered affirmatively. The judge started a Wednesday luncheon group that met regularly to talk, pray and share about the Lord.

My friend the judge had experienced God in a dynamic way at the crusade. His heart was moved and he sensed a leading from the Lord. As a result of that experience, he felt called to begin a Bible study.

The Bible describes many ways in which God calls his servants. But in those stories a pattern emerges. A specific call is usually accompanied by a revelation of God to that person. Moses met God in a burning bush ("Now then go, and I, even I, will be with your mouth..." Ex. 4:12). Gideon was visited by the angel of the Lord ("The Lord is with you, O valiant warrior." Judg. 6:12). The twelve disciples experienced a revelation of God in the flesh ("How do you know me?" -Nathanael Jn. 1:48). Paul met Jesus in a flash of blinding light ("Who are you, Lord?" Acts 9:5).

PRINCIPLE: Revelation accompanies call.

It isn't that these saints did not believe in God already or at least have some idea of Who God was. My friend, the judge, was already a believing, churchgoing Christian. But God chose to reveal Himself to him in a richer, deeper and fuller way at the time that He called him. Why?

REVELATION AND AUTHORITY

Sometimes the things that we do don't always make sense. In fact, almost everyone engages in behavior at one time or another that is downright self-defeating. If these incidents are closely examined, the cause often stems from a failure to understand and honor authority.

Mahir loved soccer and he loved his friends. He was an extremely talented athlete, and was capable of immense charm when he wished. Like many talented people, however, his character did not match his talent. Mahir simply could not seem to avoid behavior that was self-destructive.

In the middle of one soccer season, I was driving my team back from a soccer game. I was tired and so was my team. A scuffle broke out in the seat behind me. A brief check of the rearview mirror revealed that the argument involved Mahir and another player, Jallah. Mahir's involvement did not surprise me because of his quick temper.

"Guys, stop that!" I yelled, trying at the same time to keep the van on the road. "Mahir, come up here and sit beside me."

"Why are you picking on me? Why don't you tell Jallah to sit beside you?"

"Mahir, I am trying to drive this vehicle safely, and I can't have guys fighting in the van. You know the rules. I need for one of you to come ride up here and you're the one. Come on up here."

"No."

"Mahir, everyone, including you, needs to obey the rules of this team. Now please come up here or I will stop the van."

"I'm not going to do it."

At this point, I knew that I had a problem. I didn't just have a problem because Mahir was refusing to sit beside me. I had a problem because Mahir was defying the coach - the person in charge of the team. Mahir was challenging authority. Did he think I wasn't serious about my words? Did he think I didn't have the authority? Did he think he was too good a player to receive serious discipline? I didn't know, but I intended to find out.

I pulled the van off of the road, stopped it, and asked Mahir to get out and talk with me alone. He stepped out of the van. I took a deep breath before I spoke.

"Mahir," I began as gently as possible, "I am not blaming you for that argument. I don't know how it started or who is at fault. I asked you to sit beside me because I can't have fighting in the van."

"Coach," he replied, "I promise I won't fight any more. But I am not going to change seats."

"Mahir, please understand that the issue is bigger than who sits where. The issue is authority. I am the coach and I am in charge of the team. As a team member, you need to obey the rules. During a game, I can't have a player refuse to play a position or disobey me when I tell them to come out of a game. Every player has to obey the rules, or he can't be on the team."

"Coach, this isn't fair. You always pick on me."

"This matter is not about you and me. You don't have to obey me because of who I am. You need to obey me because I am in the position of coach. As long as you are on this team, you are under my authority. If you see me on the street and it's not related to the team, you can do whatever you want. You don't even have to speak to me. But if you want to remain on this team, you need to obey the rules."

"I am not going to sit beside you."

"Mahir, if you can't obey the rules, you can't be on the team. Please consider carefully because right now you are making a choice. I ask you - I beg you - please come sit in the front seat. If you choose not to do so, though, you will no longer be on the team.

Mahir paused and thought for a moment. "I'm not going to move, Coach."

"Okay, Mahir," I said sadly. "You can sit in the same seat on the way back, but you are no longer a member of this team. Turn in your uniform when we get back to the school."

Mahir climbed back into the van and reclaimed his seat. To the stunned disbelief of his teammates, he was suspended for the rest of the season.

As I thought about Mahir, I thought about what his decision cost him. He had practiced through the preseason, sweating through hundreds of sprints and drills, and running countless miles. He had trained hard with his teammates and played a number of games together with them. That effort was now wasted because he was unwilling to move three feet - three feet from the middle bench of a van to the front seat.

Mahir's actions did not make sense to me. What Jonah did really did not make much sense either. God issued a call for His prophet, Jonah, to go to Nineveh. "Arise, go to Nineveh..." Jon. 1:2.

Instead, Jonah chose to flee. He boarded a ship bound for Tarshish - which lay in a direction opposite that of Nineveh. Scripture says that Jonah fled "from the presence of the Lord." Jon. 1:3. Did Jonah think that he could outrun God? Or did he just think that he could evade God's command? Did Jonah not understand Who God Was or comprehend His authority?

Whatever the reason for Jonah's defiance, God dealt with Jonah in accordance with God's authority. He revealed Himself to Jonah.

1. THE STORM - First, God sent a great storm that battered the boat on which Jonah sailed. Jon. 1:4. This storm demonstrated God's power. God is all powerful. He is OMNIPOTENT.

2. THE LOTS - Next, the sailors cast lots to learn on whose account the storm was sent. The lot fell on Jonah. Jon. 1:7. The outcome of the lots demonstrated God's knowledge. God knows everything. He is OMNISCIENT. God exposed Jonah as the responsible party.

3. THE DEEP - When the lot fell on Jonah, he confessed his disobedience to the crew. He now understood the manner in which God was dealing with him. Jonah told the sailors to throw him

into the raging sea (Jon. 1:12), which they reluctantly did to save the boat and themselves. Jon. 1:15. Jonah sank into the depths of the sea, but cried to the Lord for mercy. "I called out of my distress to the Lord, and He answered me. I cried for help from the depth of Sheol; Thou didst hear my voice." Jon. 2:2. The fact that God answered Jonah from the depths demonstrated God's presence. God is everywhere. He is OMNIPRESENT.

Finally, God delivered Jonah from certain death. This rescue demonstrated God's SALVATION - a demonstration so profound that it is a type of Jesus' death and burial. "[A]s Jonah was three days and three nights in the belly of the sea monster, so shall the son of Man be three days and three nights in the heart of the earth." Mt. 12:40. Jonah now understood the redemptive nature of God. In the belly of the fish, he said "Salvation is from the Lord." Jon. 2:9.

God revealed Himself to Jonah. Previously, Jonah had knowledge about God. Then Jonah *experienced* Who God was. Now, Jonah truly understood the authority of the God that had called him. Now, Jehovah was his Lord.

PRINCIPLE: Revelation of God imparts the authority of the call to the disciple.

THE IMPACT OF REVELATION - PART ONE

What is the impact of revelation of God on the called disciple? When God reveals Himself to the disciple, the disciple knows Whom he represents.

Revelation resolves the issue of Lordship. Which one is the Lord? Who has the authority? The question of Lordship must be answered before the disciple can fulfill his call effectively. Through revelation of Himself to the disciple, God settles the issue of the authority of His Lordship once and for all. After His experience in the deep, Jonah knew the One Who sent him. He understood His power, His knowledge, His presence, and His salvation. "Those who regard vain idols forsake their faithfulness." Jon. 2:8.

The proof of Lordship is obedience. Who is to be obeyed? Is the disciple submitted fully

24

to the authority of the Lord? Jonah was previously disobedient. Now that he truly knew His Lord, he obeyed Him. When God called Jonah to Nineveh a second time - "Arise, go to Nineveh" (Jon. 3:2), Jonah immediately obeyed. He preached to the Ninevites with authority (Jon. 3:4), and the Ninevites repented (Jon. 3:5-10).

By contrast, the sons of Sceva were not called by God. They tried to exercise authority over demons. But God had not given them authority. They knew about Jesus and they knew the right words "I adjure you by Jesus who Paul preaches" (Acts 19:13), but they did not have a grant of God's authority. "And the evil spirit answered and said to them, 'I recognize Jesus, and I know about Paul, but **who are you**?' And the man, in whom was the evil spirit, leaped on them, and subdued all of them and overpowered them, so that they fled out of that house naked and wounded." Acts 19:15-16. The sons of Sceva did not have a revelation of the One whose authority they claimed.

"HERE AM I. SEND ME!"

I talk with many Christians who struggle with call. They do not feel that God has given them clear direction for their lives. But the question must be asked: Are we willing to obey?

Whatever the cost of the call, the disciple must be completely willing to obey and serve. It is a total yieldedness. The Lord leads at the point that the disciple is willing to follow.

The Lord revealed Himself to Isaiah in a marvelous way. "I saw the Lord sitting on a throne, lofty and exalted, with the train of His robe filling the temple." Isa. 6:1. This revelation brought Isaiah to the place of complete obedience.

"Then I heard the voice of the Lord saying, 'Whom shall I send, and who will go for Us?' Then I said, 'Here am I. Send me!" Isa. 6:8. Isaiah's response was unconditional. He was willing to be sent - anywhere...any time...to any people...to say anything. He did not express any reservations. His commitment was unqualified. The revelation of the Lord that he received was such that he had a complete willingness to obey and to serve the Master. Isaiah had reached the point of "Here am I. Send me!"

PRINCIPLE: The Lord leads at the point that the disciple is willing to follow.

REDEMPTION

Mahir received a second chance. The next year, he was allowed to return to the team. Unfortunately, he repeated the same pattern. Early that season, I dismissed him from the team for outrageous (and humiliating) actions during a game.

At the beginning of his third season, Mahir showed up confidently on the first day of tryouts. I told him that I could not allow him to try out for the team that season. His prior actions showed that he had not learned to control himself. His behavior had been detrimental to the team. Mahir was stunned. Despite a few choice words from him, I told him that I was not banning him from the team forever. If he could demonstrate a change at Sunday soccer during the off-season, I would consider letting him play the next year.

Here is the good news! Mahir played on the team during his fourth and final season. In fact, he was a team leader and a captain. And he made it through the whole season - which is a fact that Mahir now proudly recalls when I see him.

One day during that fourth and final season, Mahir was (ironically enough) riding in the front seat beside me in the van. We were talking about the past - and the history of our relationship. Mahir pointed at his head and said, "Coach, do you see my forehead?"

I glanced at Mahir quizzically. "Your forehead?"

"Yes, my forehead. Coach," Mahir proclaimed proudly, "my forehead is like a rock!"

When I think of Mahir's rebelliousness or of Jonah's flight, I shake my head in disbelief - until I consider my own actions and my own heart. "My forehead is like rock" well describes so many who claim to know the Lord and to possess His call. Yet their lives do not reflect His Lordship. Through revelation, God demonstrates His Lordship to His servant.

MEDITATION: "For the gifts and calling of God are irrevocable." Rom 11:29.

1. Do you sense the authority in this verse?

2. Is there a connection between "gifts" and "calling?"

3. Has God revealed Himself to you in any way?

4. What facets of His Nature have you experienced?

5. Do your actions demonstrate that you know His Lordship?

REVIEW:

1. To fulfill his call, the disciple must understand the authority of God.

2. Authority is the power to govern, supervise or judge a person, place or thing.

3. A call from God is a grant of His authority.

4. Revelation of God imparts the authority of the call to the disciple.

5. When God reveals Himself to the disciple, the disciple knows Whom he represents.

6. Revelation resolves the issue of Lordship.

7. The Lord leads at the point that the disciple is willing to follow.

APPLICATION: In order to fulfill the Lord's call, you must understand about His authority. The issue of Lordship must be resolved. God reveals Himself to the believer so that the believer realizes the awesome nature of the Lord he serves.

You need this knowledge for the sake of obedience. In order to fulfill your call, the Lord will direct you to do things that you do not want to do. Many aspects of service will require self-denial and self-sacrifice. These actions will conflict with your will and your nature. But prompt obedience is required.

Lordship is necessary. Lordship yields obedience in word - and in action.

REVELATION: AUTHORITY -   ATTITUDE

WHOSE...   ...LORDSHIP?   ...GLORY?

LESSON 3 – "DEPART FROM ME, FOR I AM A SINFUL MAN, O LORD!"

The church had been growing and thriving. Many of its young converts were now maturing into gifted ministers. Then the church entered a time of transition. The Senior Pastor retired and his choice for pastor replaced him. The new Senior Pastor was a wonderful, humble man of God. His heart for the congregation was evident as he poured out his life to care for his flock. Teaching, however, was not his primary gift. It is hard for one man to have the "total package." The pastoral sermons were encouraging and Biblical, but they did not contain strong teaching content.

Over the next couple of years, other members who had wonderful teaching gifts blessed the body with them. One man taught a weekly adult Sunday school brimming with well fed participants. He occasionally gave sermons on Sundays. Another lay person - a good friend of mine, was also permitted to speak at Sunday services. He was a fervent man and he delivered powerful sermons.

Then one Sunday morning, the Senior Pastor arose before the congregation. He announced a new policy: "From now on, only pastors will be allowed to give sermons on Sundays." The Sunday lay teaching stopped.

Over the next few months, the church changed. One by one, the teachers left the church. They went to other churches or even became pastors and formed their own congregations. Other members left as well - members perhaps to whom strong teaching on Sunday mornings was important. Teaching languished and church attendance dwindled.

What changed the direction of that church? There are usually different perspectives to important issues. Did "lay sermons" contaminate the integrity of the pulpit? Was the authority of the pastoral office threatened by the strong teaching gifts of others?

Why did the teachers leave the church? Did they feel that their call to teach was hampered by the exclusion from Sunday preaching? Were they offended by the new pastoral policy of the church?

Whatever the perspectives, the church lost the benefit of some strong gifts of teaching. The teachers themselves may have lost opportunities to fulfill a call from God to teach.

PRINCIPLE: Personal offense can stymie a call from God.

THE IMPACT OF REVELATION, PART TWO

Here is your assignment:

Take off all of your clothes. Take off your shoes. You are now naked and barefoot. Walk around among your friends, family and fellow citizens. Do this for three years.

Here is another assignment:

The most powerful king on earth has invaded your country. This king is on a roll. He has conquered his biggest rival. Next, he defeated numerous smaller kingdoms in the area, including your sister city. Now, he has turned his attention to your city.

The king has sent an army of over 185,000 soldiers to besiege you. This army has overwhelming superiority to anything that your city can put on the field. The city is surrounded. The king has sarcastically offered to give your own king 2,000 horses, IF your king can muster 2,000 men able to ride them and fight against his 185,000 warriors.

Now, get up, go out and loudly proclaim "This army will not even shoot an arrow at this city!"

Do you think that people laughed at this man? Surely he was the object of ridicule and derision! What type of person could fulfill these assignments? Not a person easily offended. What type of foundation would this person need to complete them? Only a person that knew in his heart of hearts that God had called him to serve God.

Isaiah is the man that God called to carry out these tasks. Is. 20:2-3; 37:33. God knew that Isaiah would need a firm foundation in God to fulfill them. So the revelation of God to

Isaiah when God called Isaiah was extraordinary:

> In the year of King Uzziah's death, I saw the Lord sitting on a throne, lofty and exalted, with the train of His robe filling the temple. Seraphim stood above him, each having six wings; with two He covered his face, and with two He covered his feet, and with two He flew. And one called out to another, and said, "Holy, holy, holy, is the Lord of hosts, the whole earth is full of His glory." And the foundations of the thresholds trembled at the voice of Him who called out, while the temple was filling with smoke. Isa. 6:1-4.

Isaiah's reaction is telling. "Woe is me, for I am ruined! Because I am a man of unclean lips and I live among a people of unclean lips; for my eyes have seen the King, the Lord of Hosts." Is. 6:5. The revelation of God shows us the truth about ourselves. It exposes our own wretched state. It is a stark realization.

This realization creates the attitude necessary to fulfill the Lord's call. It is a focus on our complete worthlessness and on His complete Worthiness. As Paul poignantly said, "For I know that nothing good dwells in me..." Rom. 7:18.

A true revelation of God does not exalt us or give us status. It doesn't make us superspiritual or somehow a cut above other believers. It is a humbling event that leaves no room for boasting, self-aggrandizement, or offense. It is an experience that makes a disciple want to fall down, touch his forehead to the ground and stay there.

Isaiah's response is similar to Peter's reaction to Jesus. Peter was confronted by the power and authority of the Lord when Jesus caused a miraculous catch of fish. "When Simon Peter saw that, he fell down at Jesus' feet, saying, 'Depart from me, for I am a sinful man, O Lord!'" Lk. 5:8. Now that Jesus had revealed Himself and Peter realized his own unworthiness, Jesus could call Peter to follow Him and to become a "fisher of men." Mt. 4:19.

PRINCIPLE: Revelation of God directs our focus away from ourselves.

The realization of our lowly state leads to humble repentance, and then by the Lord's grace, His sanctification. The Lord sanctified Isaiah's mouth. "Behold, this has touched your lips; and your iniquity is taken away, and your sin is forgiven." Isa. 6:6-7. This repentance and sanctification is a necessary preparation for the call of God.

When we meet the Lord of the universe, it changes our attitude - both our attitude about ourselves and our attitude about others. God alters our perspective, our outlook, and our values, as He begins to conform us to Himself. We understand that His glory is all that matters.

> PRINCIPLE: Revelation of God prepares us to serve God alone.

TWO ATTITUDES

Here are two candidates for spiritual leadership positions. Please select the best qualified candidate:

Qualifications of Candidate A	Qualifications of Candidate B
1. Prestigious education.	**1. Wilderness nomad.**
2. Powerful speaker.	**2. Poor speaker.**
3. Vast financial resources.	**3. Little resources**
4. Connections in high places.	**4. Marital instability.**
5. Noted for powerful deeds.	**5. Isolated existence.**
6. Highly self-assured.	**6. Low self-esteem.**
7. Leader of men.	**7. Herder of sheep.**

Which candidate would you select?

God selected Candidate B. We know that God selected Candidate B, because God dealt with Candidate A in such a way that he became Candidate B. Candidate A and Candidate B are the same person - Moses. Candidate A is Moses as he is described in scripture at age forty before he left Egypt. (Acts 7:21-22; Heb. 11:26). Candidate B is how Moses is described at age eighty around the time that God told him to return to Egypt. (Ex. 3-4). Why was Candidate B more qualified than Candidate A?

Moses knew that he was called as a Deliverer before he left Egypt! Exodus does not record this fact, but the Book of Acts does. "And when he saw one of them being treated unjustly, he defended him and took vengeance for the oppressed by striking down the Egyptian. And he supposed that his brethren understood that God was granting them deliverance through him; but they did not understand." Acts 7:24-25. But Moses was not yet equipped to be of service to the Lord Almighty. God had not yet prepared Moses to fulfill his call.

When Moses killed the Egyptian, he acted in his own flesh. He presumed that he had the ability to lead a rebellion against the Egyptians. Moses was acting in accordance with his worldly training in Pharaoh's palace. God knew that Moses was not qualified to serve the Most High!

When God revealed himself to Moses in the burning bush forty years later, Moses was a different man. He was humble and broken. Tending sheep in the wilderness for four decades was excellent training for the task of leading the people of Israel. Later, when Moses searched for a successor, he realized the need for a shepherd's heart and skill. "May the Lord, the God of the spirits of all flesh, appoint a man over the congregation, who will go out and come in before them, and who will lead them out and bring them in, that the congregation of the Lord may not be like sheep which have no shepherd." Num. 27:16-17.

In order to serve the Lord and fulfill his call, the servant of the Lord must realize that he is fully inadequate! The servant of God should not just feel inadequate. That is low self-esteem. The servant of God must know that he is fully inadequate - just like Moses at the burning bush.

PRINCIPLE: The Lord calls broken vessels.

Compare Moses as Candidate A and Candidate B with the manner in which Jesus depicts true authority to the disciples in Matthew 20. "You know that the rulers of the Gentiles lord it over them, and their great men exercise authority over them." Mt. 20:25. This description aptly describes the education and training that Moses received in Pharaoh's palace. It is illustrated by Moses' murder of the Egyptian. At that time, Moses understood leadership as power and domination.

"It is not so among you, but whoever wishes to become great among you shall be your servant, and whoever wishes to be first among you shall be your slave." Mt. 20:26-27. After forty years in the wilderness, and meeting God Almighty in the burning bush, Moses was now ready to lead Israel by serving, not by domination. Moses was now prepared to fulfill his call from God.

ANOTHER KEY ISSUE

Here is a story from a person that I know:

The worst meeting of my life occurred a few years ago.

After years of personal study and work, I sensed a clear call to teach – initially in my church. Over the next few months there unfolded a series of events that were remarkable. Words were given and doors were opened to allow me to teach in the church. It was as if the Lord moved to arrange affairs sovereignly.

After a church elders' retreat at which the Lord's presence was palpable, the elders confirmed my call to teach at the church. They had a copy of material that I had developed over many years, and decided to recommend it.

Then it happened – the worst meeting of my life. The pastors and elders met to discuss teaching direction for the body. The elders shared what had happened at the retreat and shared my call to teach. They distributed my material and recommended it.

But instead, the Pastor suggested a possible sermon series based on <u>The Purpose Driven Life</u> by Rick Warren. Another person declared that he had been given vision for the church. When asked to share that vision, he said that he alone understood the vision, and no one else. Confusion seemed to set in.

Finally, the Pastor shook his head and announced "The material here looks long and involved. It would take eighteen or twenty Sundays to teach this stuff. I planned to teach <u>The Purpose Driven Life</u>, and that is what we are going to do." And that is what the church did.

I went home stunned and dejected. Over the next few months, I had a decision to make. I felt called by God to teach our body. I shared that call and it seemed that God had arranged events sovereignly to put that call into place. But the call was not recognized by the pastors of my church. Rejection was a bitter pill to swallow.

I prayed about leaving the church. But the Lord did not release me to do so. Ultimately, I decided that I could only share my call from my perspective. I could not control whether others recognized my call, received my call, or were willing to submit to it. It was about God. It was not about me. With the rest of our church, I read The Purpose Driven Life, and I went "back to my plow" working in the ministry that I had. I never taught that material to my church.

The preparation of God, and the revelation of God, address a key issue: Whose glory is being sought? Does our work and ministry point to our own glory? Or is **all** glory given to God? "Whoever serves, let him do so as by the strength which God supplies; so that in **all** things God may be glorified through Jesus Christ, to whom belongs the glory and dominion forever and ever. Amen." I Pet. 4:11. It is about God alone, not us.

PRINCIPLE: God calls us to glorify Him alone, not ourselves.

WHOSE GLORY?

God prepared Moses to fulfill his call. For the rest of his life, Moses was very jealous for the glory of God alone. Moses experienced the glory of the Lord on Mount Sinai (Exodus 19). Moses saw the glory of the Lord from the cleft of a rock ("I pray Thee, show me Thy glory!" Ex. 33:18). He reminded Aaron of the Lord's command, "By those who come near Me I will be treated as holy, and before all the people, I will be honored." Lev. 10:3.

The children of Israel rebelled time after time in the desert. They often rejected Moses' leadership, and even intended to kill Moses. Num. 14:10. Moses could have taken offense and spurned Israel. But to do so would have destroyed the call that God had placed on Moses' life!

God offered to wipe out the rebellious children of Israel, and raise up His people from Moses alone. "I will smite them with pestilence and dispossess them, and I will make you into a nation greater and mightier people than they." Num. 14:12. Think of what God was telling Moses! "You, Moses, will be the father of My people. Forget about Abraham! You will be source of a greater and stronger nation. You will be The Man!"

If Moses had any concern for his own glory, he would have accepted this offer. But God had dealt with Moses in such a way that Moses was concerned only for the glory of God - glory that was being exalted by Moses' work. Moses knew that his call was not about him. Spurning his own glory, Moses interceded for the offending people before the Lord, falling on his face and pleading that the Lord's reputation was borne by His people. The Lord honored Moses' intercession. "So the Lord said, 'I have pardoned them according to your word; but indeed, as I live, all the earth will be filled with the glory of the Lord.'" Num. 14:20-21.

PRINCIPLE: Authority does not rejoice in power, but in God alone.

A HARSH STANDARD

Moses, the servant of the Lord ("Now the man Moses was very humble, more than any man who was on the face of the earth." Num. 12:3), was careful to honor the Lord in every situation - every situation, that is, except one. In the book of Numbers, the congregation of Israel moved from one vile rebellion to another (Num. 11, 12, 14, and 16). Then, Moses' beloved sister, Miriam, died. Num. 20:1. Immediately after Miriam's death, the people rose up against Moses and Aaron due to the lack of water. Num. 20:2.

The glory of the Lord appeared and God instructed Moses to speak to the rock and it would yield water. Moses no doubt was an emotional wreck. Instead of strictly obeying and speaking to the rock, Moses struck the rock twice with his rod (the symbol of God's authority), and cried "Listen now, you rebels; shall *we* bring forth water for you out of this rock?" Num. 20:10-11. At that moment, he and God both knew that Moses had failed to honor God before the people and in his own heart. Num. 20:12

36

PRINCIPLE: Authority glorifies God alone because He is its Source.

The consequences of this one act were dire. Because they did not honor Him as holy before the people, God informed Moses and Aaron that they would not be permitted to enter the Promised Land. Num. 20:12. Understand the impact of this sentence upon Moses. His whole life consisted of preparation and fulfillment of a call - a call that would culminate by leading the people of Israel into the Promised Land. Moses was devastated. He begged God to relent and to allow him enter the Promised Land. Deut. 3:23-28. It was the desire of his heart. But the Lord would not heed Moses' pleas and He finally told Moses, "Enough! Speak to Me no more about this matter." Deut. 3:26.

PRINCIPLE: At the point that we exalt in our authority, we are not worthy of it.

Why was the Lord's discipline on Moses so harsh? Why did He hold Moses to such a high standard? The greater the authority granted to a disciple, the greater the responsibility upon that disciple. Lk. 12:48. The greater the revelation of the glory of God, the more honor to God is required. God held Moses to a standard commensurate with his authority and revelation.

PRINCIPLE: The Lord is strict with those closest to Him.

MEDITATION: "I do not receive glory from men." Jn. 5:41.

1. Is this verse true of you?

2. How often do you think about the glory of God?

3. Is the glory of God a primary motivating factor in your life?

4. How often are you concerned with your own status?

REVIEW:

1. Personal offense can stymie a call from God.
2. Revelation of God directs our focus away from ourselves.
3. Revelation of God prepares us to serve God alone.
4. The Lord calls broken vessels.
5. God calls us to glorify Him alone, not ourselves.
6. Authority does not rejoice in power, but in God alone.
7. Authority glorifies God alone because He is its Source.
8. At the point that we exalt in our authority, we are not worthy of it.
9. The Lord is strict with those closest to Him.

SUMMARY: In order to fulfill God's call, the believer must have a heart that glorifies God and God alone. The issue of glory must be resolved. God reveals Himself to the believer so that the believer experiences the glory of the Lord he serves.

You need an unwavering desire to glorify God alone to fulfill your call. When God calls you, many people will not understand that call. I am not just speaking about the people of the world. Many Christians will reject you. They will not agree that God has called you. They will not perceive the authority of the gift(s) that God has given you to fulfill your call. This rejection will breed within you resentment, pain, and disobedience - if you have any concern for your own glory. You may even abandon your call.

God's glory is paramount. If your motivation is pure - if your sole motivation is the glory of God, you will continue to function in your call to His glory without regard to the rejection or offense of men.

REVELATION:	AUTHORITY -	ATTITUDE -	EMPOWERMENT
WHOSE...	...LORDSHIP?	...GLORY?	...STRENGTH?

LESSON 4 - "THE WAITING IS KILLING ME"

My team was riding in the van on the way to a game. It wasn't just any game. It was the final game of a long and hard fought season. I knew that it was our last game, and my team knew that it was our last game. It was the last game because it was the championship match.

Sitting beside me in the front seat was Van. Van wasn't just any player. Van was a senior and a captain of the team. He had played varsity soccer for me for four years. Van's parents were refugees from Vietnam. I had known Van since he was eight years old when he stood about as tall as my waist. I had a lot of love and respect for that guy.

But at that moment, Van was struggling. "Coach," he whispered, "I am so nervous that I can barely stand it." Van was a very experienced player and normally a calm and composed person. I looked over at Van. He was pale and doubled over as if he was holding his stomach.

Van looked back at me weakly and shook his head. "Coach," he said, "I need some help. I've never been in this type of situation before. I don't know if I am going to make it. The waiting is killing me!"

"Van," I said, "let me share a couple of things with you. First, being nervous before a big game is good. There is nothing wrong with it. It is your mind's way of preparing you for action. A little nervousness makes you alert and focused, and helps you get ready to perform. Focus and channel that energy positively, and let it help prepare you to play."

"Second, you need to understand how you will view this game in the future. You will probably remember this game for the rest of your life. We may win this game, or we may lose this game. But when you look back, you will also remember how you reacted to the game. My advice to you is to enjoy this experience. In the future, you will want to think about this game and say, 'I had a great time playing in the championship.' If you are

miserable during this game, you will probably regret that fact as much as if we lost."

I paused for a moment. "Van, today is the time of your life. Enjoy it."

Waiting for the big moment. It is a difficult thing to do. A sports championship is one thing. But what about a lifetime - waiting for your destiny in the Lord to be fulfilled? It is a slow, arduous and even painful process. Scripture tells us of many saints that received a clear call from God, but they had to wait many years for that call to be fulfilled.

Joseph had dreams as a boy. His dreams told him that he would have high positions of authority over his father and older brothers. These dreams were a call from God. Yet because of these dreams, Joseph was despised by his brothers. They planned to kill him, but sold him into slavery instead. Gen. 37.

Joseph's life went further downhill from there. Joseph became a captive in a foreign land, Egypt. Despite righteous living, he was sentenced to prison. Even after helping his friend, Pharaoh's cupbearer, interpret his own dream, Joseph was forgotten in the prison. Gen. 40. The waiting must have been unbearable. But Joseph did not lose his trust in God. His trust was not misplaced, for God was preparing Joseph for his destiny.

God knew that Joseph needed to be in Egypt to fulfill his call. He also knew that Joseph needed to be near Pharaoh at the opportune moment. So Joseph found himself in Pharaoh's prison. On one day, Joseph was languishing in prison. On the next day, Pharaoh was putting his signet ring on Joseph's hand; clothing him in fine linen; placing a gold necklace around Joseph's neck; and setting him over all the land of Egypt. Gen. 41:42-43. Joseph recognized the hand of God on his life. "God has made me lord of all Egypt." Gen. 45:9.

PRINCIPLE: The time of waiting is a time of preparation by God.

Joseph also understood God's purpose for his life when his brothers came to Egypt and bowed down before him. Through Joseph's call, God saved His people, Israel. "God sent me before you to preserve for you a remnant in the earth, and to keep you alive by a great deliverance." Gen. 45:7.

Since God has all authority on earth, He is the one that must establish authority. Even after a disciple has heard a call from God, he must wait until God sets that call in place - what is termed "empowerment." The disciple must trust that God is working to accomplish His purposes in that disciple's life. Because he waited and endured, Joseph was able to proclaim "As for you, you meant evil against me, but God meant it for good." Gen. 50:20.

PRINCIPLE: All spiritual authority is established by God alone.

JUMPING THE GUN

When I was young, my father took my brothers and me out to shoot bows and arrows. We boys loved archery. It was fun and it was challenging. Archery also fired our imaginations and, in our minds at least, helped us to identify more closely with one of our heroes, Robin Hood, and his Merry Men.

So the Merry Men sallied forth to the archery contest. Before the Merry Men could shoot, though, the Ranger of Sherwood Forest (my father) gave strict safety instructions for the archery contest. One of those instructions was that every person needed to finish shooting all his arrows before we could retrieve the arrows from the targets (or wherever else they might happen to land). The Ranger did not - and he emphasized this point - did not want any of the Merry Men to run out in front of the shooting line prematurely and get shot.

The Merry Men started shooting arrows at the targets. We were having a ball. It wasn't that the targets were being hit, but a few of the arrows did land in the general vicinity. One of the Merry Men shot all his arrows, and ran to get them. He did not think to check the other archers. Not all of the arrows had been fired. The Ranger called him back and delivered a stern lecture to us all. We were now fully warned. If the violation occurred again, the archery would stop.

The contest continued and the excitement mounted. One of the Merry Men actually hit a target! Thrilled, he jumped in the air and ran to see exactly how close to the bull's-eye he had come. Unfortunately, not all of the arrows had been shot. Within a few moments, exhilaration turned into despair as the Ranger informed the Merry Men that the Archery Contest had just been canceled.

I will never forget the feeling of deep, deep disappointment as we walked home carrying our now useless bows and arrows.

From our perspective, we were eager to shoot bows and arrows. We had been told we could do it, and it was something that we really wanted to do.

The reality, though, is that the restriction on waiting until all arrows had been shot was for our good. It was a rule imposed by authority for our own protection and well-being.

Scripture is full of examples of saints that were called by God to a task or a ministry, but they jumped the gun before God had empowered them to fulfill it. Abram had a wondrous promise from God. God called Abram to be a father - a father with descendants as numerous as the stars in the nighttime sky. Gen. 15:5.

God confirmed His call to Abram. He revealed His power and glory to Abram. God caused His presence to pass between Abram's offering in the form of a "smoking oven and a flaming torch." Gen. 15:17. In fact, he changed Abram's name to Abraham - "father of a multitude." Gen. 17.

Abraham had a problem, though. He had no children. His wife, Sarah, was barren. Even though God had revealed His power and majesty to Abraham, Abraham decided that God needed a little help. At the insistence of his wife, Abraham conceived a son with Sarah's Egyptian handmaid, Hagar. Gen. 16.

This son, Ishmael, however, was produced in Abraham's own strength. God made it clear to Abraham that Ishmael was not the promised seed. Gen. 17:18-21. Abraham loved Ishmael, but Ishmael became a thorn in Sarah's side, and a type of those who persecute God's chosen. "But as at that time he who was born according to the flesh persecuted him who was born according to the Spirit, so it is now also." Gal. 4:29. Abraham's attempt to fulfill God's call in his own strength brought him and Sarah much grief.

PRINCIPLE: Empowerment to fulfill a call of God comes in God's time and at His discretion.

WHOSE STRENGTH?

The time of waiting for empowerment from God addresses another core issue: By whose strength will the ministry be established? Will the disciple try to operate in his own gifts and talents, or will he wait and let God establish the call in God's strength? It is an issue of timing and it is an issue of power.

In the story about archery and shooting arrows, there is one more perspective to consider -that of my father - the Ranger. He had charge over our archery and over our lives. He made us wait to retrieve arrows and to shoot again for our own safety. When we violated his rules in our eagerness, we disregarded his authority. As a result, he revoked our ability to shoot arrows.

Desperate times require desperate measures.

What do you do when you have an army of 3,000, and your enemy has 30,000 chariots, 6,000 cavalry, and infantry that is "like the sand which is on the seashore in abundance?"

You try to be patient and wait on the Lord. You wait seven days, but His prophet doesn't come at the appointed time to offer sacrifices as promised. You are a new king, and haven't really established yourself in the people's eyes. God did reveal Himself to you mightily after you were anointed king. His Spirit fell upon you so mightily that you started prophesying. But what relatively few people you have with you are now leaving and scattering. Surely you must act and do something!

Saul faced a dilemma. I Sam. 13. What could he do to salvage the situation? He acted in accordance with his heart. He acted like a king. He acted presumptuously. Saul assumed the priestly office for himself and personally offered the sacrifices in the presence of the people. I Sam. 13:9. And as soon as the sacrifices were finished, Samuel came walking down the road and upbraided him:

You have acted foolishly; you have not kept the commandment of the Lord your God, which He commanded you: for now the Lord would have established your kingdom over Israel forever. But now your kingdom shall not endure. The Lord has sought out for Himself a man after His own heart, and the Lord has appointed him as ruler over His people, because you have not kept what the Lord commanded you. I Sam. 13:13-14.

PRINCIPLE: A man after God's own heart acts only in God's strength and God's authority.

THE ESTABLISHMENT OF GOD'S AUTHORITY

Self-defense is an absolute defense. If you shoot an unarmed man, it is murder. But if that man is armed and trying to kill you, you can shoot back. No one will hold you responsible for that man's life. That killing is justified.

And what if that man has tried to kill you a number of times before? He has hunted you "like a dog" and has told everyone around him that he wants to kill you.

Even more, the man trying to kill you has something that is rightfully yours. God told you that you would be king. God's prophet anointed you as king, and clearly proclaimed that you are the rightful king. God confirmed that anointing with a mighty presence of His Holy Spirit. And now the man who wants to remain as king and who is trying to kill you, is within your grasp.

The man that God found after His own heart was a remarkable man. David had every justification to take out Saul and seize the kingdom for himself. Not only had Saul tried to kill David, Saul even had murdered God's priests who had assisted David. This crime was so heinous that Saul's own servants would not obey Saul's order to carry out the execution. I Sam. 22:11-19.

David had two occasions where he had Saul's life within his grasp. On one occasion,

Saul was using the bathroom in a cave. I Sam. 24. On the other, Saul was asleep. I Sam. 26. One thrust of David's sword would have ended it all. David's companions urged him to do it! I Sam. 26:8; 24:4. But David understood authority. He had such respect for the anointing of the Lord that he refused to touch Saul. "Far be it from me *because of the Lord* that I should do this thing to my lord, the Lord's anointed, to stretch out my hand against him, since he is the Lord's anointed." I Sam. 24:6.

David's respect for authority was so great that he even felt pangs of conscience when he cut off the edge of Saul's robe in the cave. I Sam. 24:5. David respected the Lord and His authority. He was willing to wait until God established his call in God's strength.

> PRINCIPLE: A person in authority respects authority. He does not damage other spiritual authority to establish his own authority.

WAITING FOR GOD

God told you that you would be king. God's prophet anointed you as king, and clearly proclaimed that you are the rightful king. God confirmed that anointing with a mighty presence of His Holy Spirit.

The man who lorded his authority over you and abused you has now been killed by his enemies. I Sam. 31. You had nothing to do with his death. You have waited for years to become king.

Miraculously, a messenger delivers into your hand the crown and bracelet of that king a few days later. II Sam. 1:10. You don't put on these crown jewels, even though they were a gift.

Isn't it about time for a royal announcement?

David did not make an announcement. He did something "other worldly." He inquired of the Lord. II Sam. 2:1. The Lord told him to go to the city of Hebron.

In obedience to the Lord, David went to Hebron. II Sam. 2:1. The men of Judah then **came to him** and anointed him king over them. II Sam. 2:4. David did not try to declare himself as king of Israel, but remained king of Judah for over seven years. II Sam. 2:11.

Finally, after over seven years, "all the tribes of Israel **came to** David at Hebron" and asked him to become king over them. II Sam. 5:1-5. David was anointed and, at that point, he finally became king of Israel in Jerusalem. II Sam. 5:5.

David submitted to God's call, God's strength, and God's authority. David allowed God alone to establish his kingdom in God's time. Later, David had a realization similar to that of Joseph: "And David realized that the Lord had established him as king over Israel." II Sam. 5:12.

In order to fulfill your call, you must wait for God to empower you. The issue of strength must be resolved. God may call you to a ministry long before God empowers you to fulfill it. If you act in your own strength, you will fail. Even worse, it is presumption like Saul.

Complete trust is necessary to fulfill your call. God will accomplish His word and His work in His time. Don't act until God says "It is time." You can't force your ministry or authority on others. God's servant allows God to act, and watches in wondrous amazement as God establishes the authority of the call through His power.

> PRINCIPLE: Empowerment occurs when authority
> has been properly and fully established by God.

THE ETERNAL KINGDOM

What is the impact of David allowing God to establish his kingdom, instead of David doing it by his own strength? A kingdom established by man does not endure. David's kingdom, however, was not just a thirty-three year reign in Jerusalem.

David's kingdom is an eternal kingdom. "Your house and your kingdom shall endure before me forever; your throne shall be established forever." II Sam. 7:16. If David had murdered Saul, or taken steps to establish his kingdom by his own hand, he would have missed the blessing of an eternal kingdom established by God! Because David waited and allowed God to establish his authority, his kingdom will now last forever!

"He will be great, and will be called the Son of the Most High; and the Lord God will give Him the throne of his father David." Lk. 1:32.

PRINCIPLE: Authority established by God has eternal impact.

If you are patient and obedient, and if you allow God to establish your call in His strength and in His timing, then your work in the Kingdom of God will have eternal impact.

MEDITATION: "And He went down with them and came to Nazareth; and He continued in subjection to them; and His mother treasured all these things in her heart. And Jesus kept increasing in wisdom and stature, and in favor with God and men." Lk. 2:51-52.

1. Jesus was God in the flesh. But He waited thirty years to perform a "three year ministry." Why?

2. Paul had an emphatic call, but he waited years until God established his apostleship. See Gal. 1:19; 2:1-2. Why?

3. "And I was with you in weakness and in fear and in much trembling." I Cor. 2:3. To what extent did Paul minister out of "weakness"? Why?

4. To what areas of ministry has God called you?

5. Were you ever discouraged because your authority in those areas of ministry was not recognized?

6. "For I determined to know nothing among you except Jesus Christ, and Him crucified." I Cor. 2:2. Why did Paul describe his ministry to the Corinthians in this way?

REVIEW:

1. The time of waiting is a time of preparation by God.

2. All spiritual authority is established by God alone.

3. Empowerment to fulfill a call of God comes in God's time and at His discretion.

4. A man after God's own heart acts only in God's strength and God's authority.

5. A person in authority respects authority. He does not damage other spiritual authority to establish his own authority.

6. Empowerment occurs when authority has been properly and fully established by God.

7. Authority established by God has eternal impact.

THIS WORD IS IMPORTANT:

This book is about your call. This book (and the other books of the series The Call) have been written to help explore your call and to find your place in the body of Christ – or at least to give you a context within which to discover it.

Before going further though, please be clear about your first and primary calling. Although the last three chapters discussed call, you may have noticed that the focus of those chapters was God. Not only is He the Source of call, but He is our All in All.

God may call you to work, to ministry, to family and/or to occupation. But your first and primary calling can be summarized in two simple but profound words: "Follow Me!" Seek Him. Pursue Him. Listen to Him. Share with Him. Observe Him. Imitate Him. Yield to Him. Worship Him. Journey with Him. Grow in Him. Abide in Him. "Follow Me!"

Call arises from "Follow Me!" Life direction comes after "Follow Me!" First, we follow Him. Then, as we become conformed to Him and His likeness within us, He sends us. "Follow Me, and I will make you fishers of men." Mt. 4:19. He commissions us when we are ready and He is willing. But first there is usually a **season** of simply "Follow Me!" This last chapter described some of those seasons of waiting and following Jesus prior to launch.

But "Follow Me!" never loses its place as our first and primary call. Even after we have been called to action, empowered, sent and established, the work and ministry never displace "Follow Me!" Our call from Him will develop, adjust, and clarify as we obey it. Those transitions arise from "Follow Me!" But "Follow Me!" never stops if for no other reason because it is primary. It is the key to our identity in Him. If it ceases or even if it just becomes secondary, then we have lost our way and we have lost ourselves.

"For the vision is yet for the appointed time;

It hastens toward the goal, and it will not fail.

Though it tarries, wait for it;

For it will certainly come, it will not delay." Hab. 2:3.

SECTION TWO

STEPS TO FULFILLMENT OF CALL

Preface to Section Two

In the first four chapters of this book, we have reviewed ways in which the Lord dealt with His servants prior to establishing their call. These chapters describe Preparation for Call. They detail the character and attitudes needed to serve our Lord.

To serve God Almighty, the disciple must have settled the core issues of Lordship, glory, and strength. Daily, the disciple should discern his motivation, and should seek revelation of God.

We now turn our attention to Steps to Fulfillment of Call. In this section, we will explore the means by which the Lord wondrously works to fulfill His call in the lives of His servants.

The underlying premise is that Jesus has a work for each follower in His Kingdom. Jesus' basic instruction was to make disciples - even more, to make disciples who make disciples [See The Call - Book One (Functional)]. These next five chapters describe the steps to fulfill this work, and they elaborate each step. God sends His followers (Lesson 5) with His direction (Lesson 6) to make contact for the purpose of sharing with others (Lesson 7); for the purpose of caring for others (Lesson 8); and for the purpose of preparing others for ministry (Lesson 9). These steps are stages in the cycle of discipleship. (Study the Chart on the next page.) Thus, each step of this progression is essential.

THE CYCLE OF DISCIPLESHIP

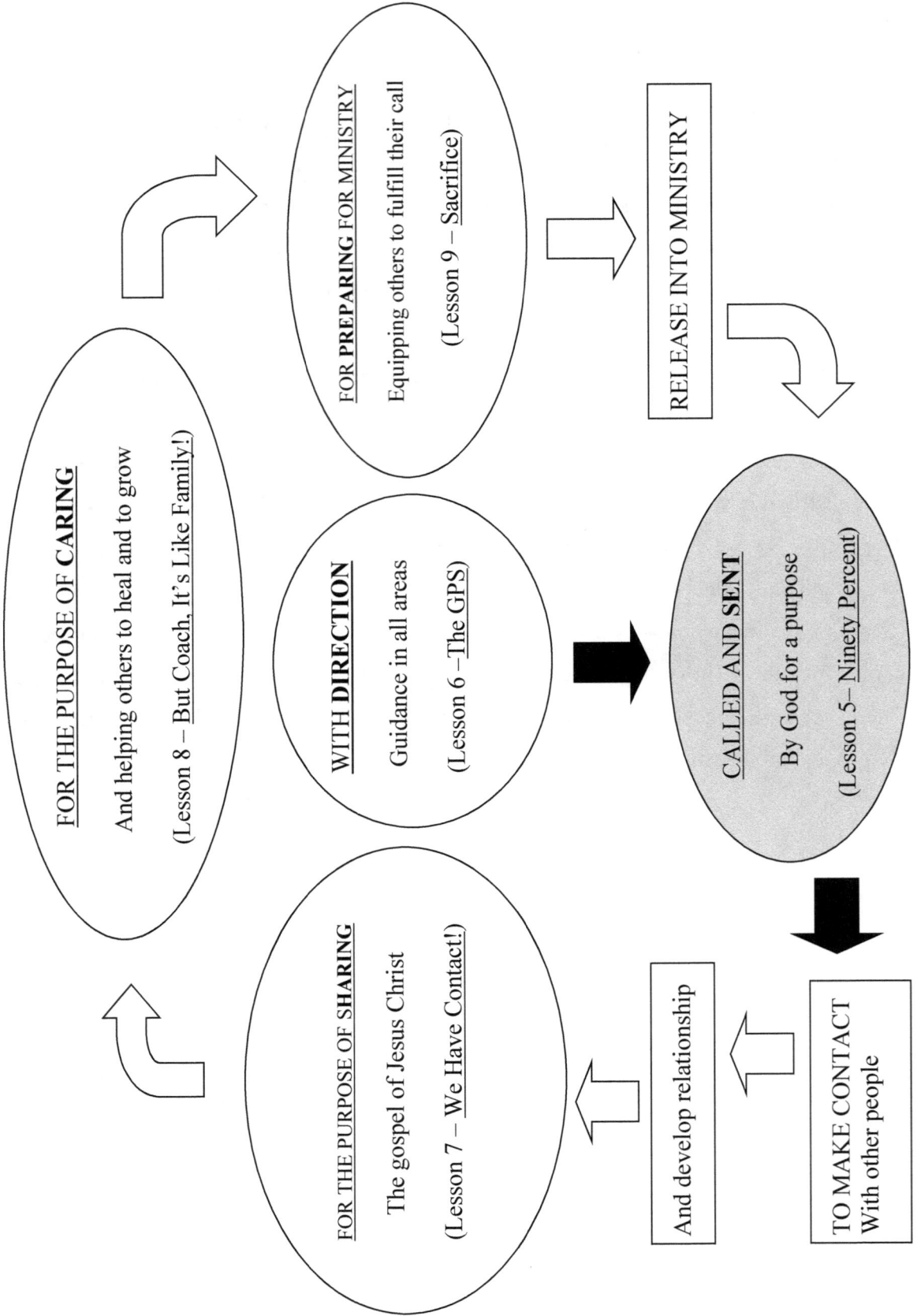

FOR PREPARING FOR MINISTRY

Equipping others to fulfill their call

(Lesson 9 – Sacrifice)

RELEASE INTO MINISTRY

FOR THE PURPOSE OF CARING

And helping others to heal and to grow

(Lesson 8 – But Coach, It's Like Family!)

WITH DIRECTION

Guidance in all areas

(Lesson 6 –The GPS)

CALLED AND SENT

By God for a purpose

(Lesson 5– Ninety Percent)

FOR THE PURPOSE OF SHARING

The gospel of Jesus Christ

(Lesson 7 – We Have Contact!)

And develop relationship

TO MAKE CONTACT
With other people

LESSON 5 - "NINETY PERCENT OF WHAT I DO IS JUST SHOW UP"

Kennedy was a relational young man. He loved people, and people loved him. Kennedy was funny and fun-loving. Kennedy possessed charm.

One evening not long after the Lord had changed his life, I received a telephone call from Kennedy. "Coach" he whispered, "I'm here at school. Something has changed." His voice had a tone of concern.

"What is it?" I asked.

"Well, coach, people are treating me different here at college. I don't know what it is. They keep their distance like they are showing me respect or something. But it also is like they are avoiding me. I don't understand." Kennedy sounded hurt.

I prayed silently before I responded. "Kennedy, let me share something with you. Listen closely. Light shines in the midst of darkness. Wherever you go, you bear the light. Darkness is afraid of the light. It is reproved by it."

I paused. It was quiet on the other end of the phone.

"Kennedy" I continued, "I think that what you are experiencing is the reaction to what the others at the school see in you. But that reaction is good, Kennedy. Whether or not others realize it, it means that they see Jesus in you."

During the next week, I had lunch with Kennedy. "Coach," he said, "you wouldn't believe what happened to me yesterday!"

"Really?" I asked. "What happened?"

"Well, I was standing outside of my class. An older woman walked up to me. She must have been eighty years old. Maybe she decided to go back to school or something. Anyway, she walked up to me and told me I was bright."

"What did you say?"

"I didn't really know what to say. I just said 'Thank you' or something like that. But, coach, you won't believe what she said next."

"What did she say?"

"She said she was trying to help some of the students. Then she said 'I am trying to bring some light into the darkness.' I couldn't believe it after what you said last week."

"Wow!"

"Then she looked at me and said, 'I am not talking about you. You are already bright.' Then she walked away."

"Kennedy, do you know this woman?"

"Coach, I have never seen this woman before or since. She isn't in any of my classes. I couldn't believe what she said!"

Light shines in the midst of darkness.

John tells us of the light of Jesus. "In Him was life; and the life was the light of men. And the light shines in the darkness; and the darkness did not comprehend it." Jn. 1:4-5.

Jesus identified His disciples as the light of the world. "You are the light of the world. A city set on a hill cannot be hidden. Nor do men light a lamp, and put it under a basket, but on the lampstand; and it gives light to all who are in the house. Let your light shine before men in such a way that they may see your good works, and glorify your father who is in heaven." Mt. 5:14-16.

Light must shine in darkness.

PRINCIPLE: Light is effective only when it shines in darkness.

In Charlotte, North Carolina, there are pockets of poverty. Instead of one large area of lower income housing, the poor of the city live in clusters of destitution. Ironically, some of the wealthiest neighborhoods of the city are situated next door to some of the poorest.

My church is located near one of these pockets of poverty. My church has ministered in this area for many years. One of the most important things my church did was to lease two apartments in the area and use them for ministry. It is not necessarily economical. The church's apartments are literally a few hundred yards from the church. The church leadership could have said "Just come to us. We are only a short walk away."

Instead, my church said "We are coming to you. We want to be a part of your neighborhood. We are interested in you."

The difference between these two approaches is huge.

PRINCIPLE: Light must go to the darkness so that light can shine in darkness.

WHY DOES GOD ISSUE A CALL?

God is a sending God. He is a God of mission. That is His nature, and that is the nature that He imparts to His disciples. They are the sending, and they are the sent. Throughout history, God has directed His followers to "Go!" God told Abraham - "Go!" (Gen. 12:1). God told Moses - "Go!" (Ex. 4:12).

Finally, and perhaps most importantly, Jesus told His disciples - "Go!" (Mt. 28:19). Being sent is a basic tenet of discipleship. When Jesus first called His disciples, He "called His disciples to Him and chose twelve of them, *whom He also named as apostles...*" Lk. 6:13. The word "apostle" literally means "one sent from (or sent away)." Jesus chose twelve disciples, but immediately informed them that they were destined to be sent.

Mk. 3:14-15 describes Jesus' call of His disciples differently: "And He appointed twelve, that they might be with Him, and that He might send them to preach, and to have authority to cast out the demons." Jesus appointed twelve for the purpose that "they might be with Him" (Discipleship); for the purpose that they "have authority to cast out demons" (Empowerment); and for the purpose "that He might send them to preach" (Apostleship).

From their first day as followers, the twelve knew that they would be sent - sent as light in the midst of darkness.

PRINCIPLE: Discipleship implies being commissioned.

Each time God called a person in scripture, He sent that person for a reason. God had a specific purpose that He wanted to accomplish on earth. He sent His servant to accomplish that purpose. Discipleship implies being sent with authority from God for His intended purpose!

When God sends a person, He may send that person to a place - a city or region; to an organization; or to a position. God's mission, however, focuses on people - specific persons or a group of people. When Jesus sent His twelve disciples, He sent them to "the lost sheep of the house of Israel." Mt. 10:6. Jesus was unequivocal in this instruction. "Do not go in the way of the Gentiles, and do not enter any city of the Samaritans..." Mt. 10:5.

We later see a clear delineation between the call of God to Peter and the call of God to Paul. "But on the contrary, seeing that I had been entrusted with the gospel to the uncircumcised, just as Peter with the gospel to the circumcised...James and Cephas and John, who were reputed to be pillars, gave to me and Barnabas the right hand of fellowship, that we might go to the Gentiles, and they to the circumcised." Gal. 2:7-9. Just as God called Peter to the Jews, He called Paul to the Gentiles.

PRINCIPLE: Through His call, God sends His saints.

QUALIFICATION TO BE SENT

A true testimony from a friend who has been sent by God to the inner city:

Recently, I had a dream. In the dream, I was standing on some type of platform overlooking land that was not familiar to me, but in the dream it was where I lived. I was rebuking Satan in the name of Jesus and praying for God's blessing over the land and the property. "Satan, I command you to leave in the name of Jesus. By the blood of Jesus you have to go. You are rebuked!" At the end of the dream I started to get scared. I knew that I was stirring up the enemy.

And then I woke up. But when I woke up, I had the same fear as in the dream. This happens to me from time to time in my house. Often I wake up and see someone outside, smoking crack cocaine, or urinating on my property, or banging on a neighbor's door or

window for them to let this person in. And so I prayed the same thing as in my dream. "Jesus, I pray that you would cleanse this house and property of evil in the mighty name of Jesus. I pray you would protect us from evil. I pray for all the men on the property and in the ministry. Satan, I rebuke you in the name of Jesus. I command you to be bound and chained and cast back into the pit of hell where you came from, in the name and by the blood of Jesus!"

I was walking around inside the house praying like this and opening the shades to look outside because I suspected that something was going on. It was about 2:15 a.m. by this time. And I did see something outside.

I saw two men walking across our property. I had to check it out. I went outside with my cell phone and my dog. The men were two of our guys. They said that the police had been there and had just left after arresting a man on our property. The man had been drinking and threatening several of our participants at the same time that I had been dreaming and rebuking the devil. It all worked out, but the situation could have been explosive. One man can cause a lot of damage when the enemy gets him in his grasp, and this unruly man was in the devil's grasp.

I laughed because the Lord has often reminded me that ninety percent of what I do is just show up - just being there. What amazed me was that even in my sleep, God used me. By the time I woke up, the incident was already over! What an awesome God we serve! And to think that He lets us participate in His work, even in our sleep! Now that is humbling!

God can handle whatever your situation is right now, and He may not even need you to be awake! But evidently He does want our prayers!

"Ninety percent of what I do is just show up!" So many times we think we need huge gifts or gigantic faith to do the work of the Lord. But the faith is in the going. The gifts arise through the Holy Spirit within you as the need arises day by day. In my friend's case, the gifts arose when he was asleep!

Being sent by God to be at the right place at the right time. When that occurs, then we can participate in the work and purpose of God.

DARKNESS RESISTS THE LIGHT

My church has had an active worship dance ministry for years. The ministry hosts week long dance camps semiannually. At the end of each camp, a worship recital is offered. Christians from all over the city gather to watch dancers perform upon the stage in the church auditorium.

One summer, the dance leaders were inspired to reach the community around the church. Instead of staging the recital in the church, the leaders wanted to hold a public recital for the neighborhood. They decided to move the recital to the church parking lot and to make it a community event. I was excited to see what would happen.

What happened was a thunderstorm! About two hours before the recital, a deluge of rain driven by nearly tornadic winds descended upon the workers in the parking lot scrambling to set up a sound system and a staging tent. Preparation became frantic. Many prayers were offered. The storm ended thirty minutes before the scheduled performance.

At the recital, I watched as talented dancers, who were accustomed to studio conditions, performed leaps and twirls on asphalt that was wet and slick from the rain. I watched as one dancer slipped and bloodied his knee. I watched another dancer lose his footing and fall hard on his elbow. The venue was inconvenient and dangerous - all because the performance had been moved seventy-five feet into the parking lot.

At the end of the performance, though, an altar call was given by one of the dance leaders. As the invitation went forth, a number of hands were raised in response. The willingness of the dancers to reach out was honored by the presence of the Lord - the presence of the Lord working in the hearts of guests in attendance.

It struck me that the outdoor dance recital was a parable of what happens when the Lord sends His saints. Moving a few feet - even with the venue still on church property - completely changed the dynamic of the dance recital. It changed from comfort to challenge.

Being sent can be a very unsettling dynamic. When God sends His servant, that servant usually leaves a comfortable setting and goes to a very discomfiting one.

I had a conversation one day with a grandmother in my church. She was deeply concerned. Her granddaughter, Mona, was a young adult. Mona participated regularly in the inner city outreach not far from the church. Mona helped with a Good Shepherd Club for young children that met weekly in one of our apartments. The neighborhood was not savory, and had a high crime rate that included violence, murder, and drug trafficking.

"I wish Mona would not go work in that neighborhood" Grandmother said. "It is far too dangerous for a young woman like Mona."

Darkness resists the light. "For everyone who does evil hates the light, and does not come to the light, lest his deeds should be exposed." Jn. 3:20. Being sent by God to be light in the midst of darkness is very uncomfortable. "If the world hates you, you know that it has hated Me before it hated you." Jn. 15:18. Yet God sends us out to be light all the same.

> PRINCIPLE: God sends His followers beyond their comfort zone.

ARE YOU WILLING TO GO?

Pastor Late is a beloved man of God who fathered many spiritual children. He regularly exhorted us, "Like Peter did, we are fond of saying that we will die for the Lord. But the question is not whether we will die for Him. The question is whether we will live for Him! If we are not living for Him now, and carefully obeying everything He tells us to do, then we are not willing to die for Him. We demonstrate our willingness to die for Him every day that we die to ourselves and conduct our lives for His glory. Otherwise, it is just idle talk."

How uncomfortable was Jeremiah? How rejected, spurned, scorned and castigated was he?

O Lord, Thou hast deceived me, and I was deceived; Thou hast overcome me and prevailed. I have become a laughingstock all day long; Everyone mocks me. For each time I speak, I cry aloud; I proclaim violence and destruction, because for me the word of the Lord has resulted in reproach and derision all day long. But if I say, "I will not remember Him or speak any more in His name," then in my heart it becomes like a burning fire shut up in my bones; and I am weary of holding it in, and I cannot endure it. Jer. 20:7-9.

Jeremiah struggled with His call. But the Lord bestowed on Jeremiah mighty authority when He called him. "Behold, I have put My words in your mouth. See, I have appointed you this day over the nations and over the kingdoms, to pluck up and to break down, to destroy and to overthrow, to build and to plant." Jer. 1:9-10. In Jeremiah 25, Jeremiah spoke the word of the Lord. In eleven verses (Jer. 25:15-26), he prophesied with authority the ruin and downfall of the kingdoms of Judah, Egypt, Uz, the Philistines, Edom, Moab, Ammon, Tyre, Sidon, Dedan, Tema, Buz, Arabia, Zimri, Elam, Media, and Babylon.

And it came to pass just as Jeremiah spoke.

MEDITATION: "Behold, I send you out as sheep in the midst of wolves." Mt. 10:16.

1. Has God ever sent you with a purpose?

2. If so, how comfortable was that experience?

3. Do you believe that personal safety is a Kingdom value?

4. "Ninety percent of what I do is just show up!" What are the implications of that statement?

5. Do you feel that God may be nudging you to minister to certain persons or a group of people?

6. Are there current comforts to which you cling that may present a barrier to a response to God's leading?

REVIEW:
1. Light is effective only when it shines in darkness.
2. Discipleship implies being commissioned.
3. Through His call, God sends His saints.
4. When we are sent by God, then we can participate in the work and purpose of God.
5. Darkness resists the light.
6. God sends His followers beyond their comfort zone.

THE CYCLE OF DISCIPLESHIP

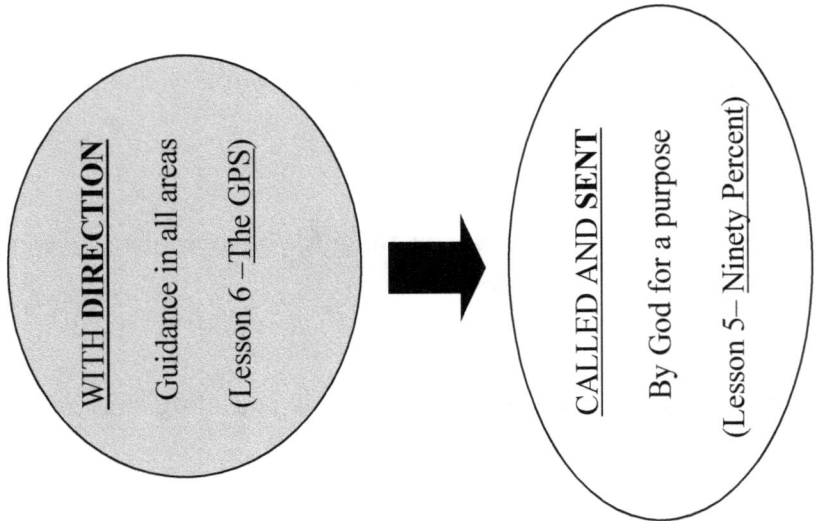

WITH DIRECTION

Guidance in all areas

(Lesson 6 – The GPS)

CALLED AND SENT

By God for a purpose

(Lesson 5 – Ninety Percent)

THE CYCLE: SENT BY GOD WITH DIRECTION

LESSON 6 - THE GPS

Twenty-five years ago, my home church was a suburban church. It catered to middle and upper class families. The church had seen phenomenal growth as members experienced a touch of the Holy Spirit in fresh and deep outpourings.

But the demographics of the city of Charlotte changed. As Charlotte grew, the inner city pushed the suburbs further out of the city and away from the church. Many of the neighborhoods surrounding the church "went down" as richer families moved out and poorer families moved in. The housing around the church developed a flavor that was mixed in race, nationality and culture.

A visionary group within the church wanted to move. Since many church members had moved to the suburbs, the church should move as well. This group found a large tract of centrally located property miles away and began to urge the church to move elsewhere and to build.

Leadership of the church reviewed its ministry, and corporately prayed for guidance. All indicators pointed toward a move - economics, facilities and demographics. In human terms, the decision seemed like a "no-brainer." But as leadership sought direction from the Lord, a word came forth: "I have called this church to be a lighthouse in the place where it is located."

The leadership of the church confirmed this guidance, and a vote of the membership affirmed it. The church decided to stay in the same place. A number of members who had wanted to move left the body soon thereafter. The church struggled with the changes that decision implied.

For me personally, that word was momentous. A few years later, I attended a church Vacation Bible School in apartments near the church. Then I personally experienced a call from the Lord that changed my life.

Guidance and direction from the Lord. This area is necessary, but it is perhaps the most difficult aspect of the Christian walk. I regularly speak with Christians that struggle to understand God's direction for their lives. His direction is the mandate for our service. Every follower of Jesus should spend time with Him, and daily seek His will for his or her life.

Guidance from the Lord is the key to receiving, understanding and fulfilling the call of the Lord in our lives. Through revelation from the Holy Spirit, we learn the necessary details - where to go; when to do it; to whom to minister; how to go about it; and what to say. Revelation is the GPS of ministry. Revelation shows us the direction to go, and keeps us from getting lost on the way.

PRINCIPLE: Through guidance, the Lord communicates His call.

ALWAYS LISTENING

Scripture directs Jesus' followers to go into the world and bear witness. Paul himself told Timothy to be ready to preach the word "in season and out of season." II Tim. 4:2. Paul functioned in this mode continuously. The Lord had called him to preach the gospel to the Gentiles. Gal. 2:7.

Yet at one point, Paul and his coworkers were in Asia. Paul wanted to preach the gospel in Asia. But Paul was "forbidden by the Holy Spirit to speak the word in Asia!" Acts 16:6. They tried to go minister in Bithynia, but "the Spirit of Jesus did not permit them!" Acts 16:7. How amazing! Through guidance of the Holy Spirit, Paul and his coworkers were forbidden to do the very thing that scripture commands, and the very thing that God had called them to do!

Instead, the Lord wanted Paul to cross over into Europe. He revealed His will to Paul in a vision. Acts 16:9. How did Paul and his coworkers know when to speak or when not to speak? How did they know where to go and where not to go? Only through revelation were they able to understand and obey the work that God had ordained - for the gospel to be preached in Europe!

It is important to use our intellect. God has given us a mind to use, and we should use it fully. In fact, He instructs us to love Him with all of our mind. Mk. 12:30. Yet God says that His thoughts are not our thoughts, and His ways are not our ways. His thoughts are higher than our thoughts, and His ways are higher than our ways. Isa. 55:8-9.

Many Christians function in a default mode. Those Christians apply their minds to scripture, and set their ways accordingly.

Sometimes, though, God grants further revelation. He directs us in various ways - through circumstances, dreams, a sensing, a Voice, a word from other Christians or through the illumination of scripture. God gives us guidance beyond our ordinary function. This guidance shows us the right way - the right direction for a time, an event or a circumstance. This guidance reveals His will to us.

For this reason, every Christian should be seeking direction from the Lord every day. We function in accordance with scripture and in accordance with our understanding of Christian action. But we remain open to a "higher way" from the Lord. Isa. 55:9. Our spiritual ears are always listening. My church understood one direction through applied wisdom. But only by seeking the Lord was a higher way revealed.

PRINCIPLE: God sends His people with direction.

THE IMPACT OF DIRECTION

I once visited the Civil War battlefield of Antietam. The battlefield stretches for miles - a place where long columns comprised of over 100,000 soldiers met each other in desperate combat. Casualty estimates from one day of warfare approach 23,000. More Americans lost their lives that day than on any other single day of combat in the history of the United States.

General A.P. Hill of the Confederacy began the morning of the battle with his troops at Harper's Ferry, some seventeen miles away from Antietam. At 6:30 AM that morning, General Hill received orders to bring as many soldiers as he could to Antietam as quickly as possible. Within an hour, General Hill set out with his units on an exhausting march to Antietam.

The battle of Antietam rolled across the front lines throughout the day as the two armies tried to outflank each other. In the morning, the fighting started on the northern portion of the battlefield at the "Bloody Cornfield" and Dunker Church. By midday, the battle had moved south to the middle of the armies where thousands of brave men lost their lives at the Sunken Road. The slaughter was so great that the road is forever remembered as "Bloody Lane." Fighting at each section of the battlefield subsided only due to the exhaustion, shock and casualty of the soldiers.

By the early afternoon, the Union forces mounted an attack on the southern portion of the battlefield. The Union charge gained momentum, and the army surged forward, pushing the Confederates back. By 3:30 that afternoon, the Confederate position was in severe jeopardy. Their columns had broken and were in full retreat. If the Union forces could turn the Confederate flank and roll up the line, Robert E. Lee's whole army might be destroyed, and with it, the hopes of the Confederacy. The Confederate army was in a desperate situation.

Then, "up came Hill." At that moment, at 3:30 that afternoon, A.P. Hill arrived with 3,500 exhausted, but battle fresh soldiers. Assessing the situation quickly, General Hill committed his charges to the fray immediately without waiting for orders. His troops held their position, then beat back the Union assault. The arrival of Hill's troops saved the Confederate army.

"Up came Hill" became a byword for the army. From that point on, whenever any soldier, unit or army performed a heroic feat in which just the right action was taken at just the right time, it was "up came Hill." It meant salvation.

"Up came Hill" describes the impact of revelation. The Holy Spirit is perfect in His timing, His word and His action. Salvation does not occur by accident. Guidance from the Holy Spirit is the variable that distinguishes the glorious work of the Lord and the ineffectual work of man. It is the difference between victory and defeat.

Guidance is the compass of the disciple. It is the lynchpin that binds together all that we do. My encouragement is to seek and to keep on seeking. "You will seek me and find me when you search for Me with all your heart." Jer. 29:13.

PRINCIPLE: The Lord gives perfect direction for His work.

DYNAMICS OF GUIDANCE

Guidance by the Holy Spirit is necessary for effective Christian ministry. Yet guidance is an area that spooks many believers. Insecurity, fear of mistake, and selfishness hinder many saints and prevent them from seeking revelation.

Furthermore, there is no set formula. Revelation is not something that another person can do for you. To quote a friend, "no one else can be the Holy Spirit in your life." The Lord speaks differently to each person in each situation. Different circumstances require different directions. Here are a few keys to guidance, and a few cautions.

A. The first key to revelation is a state of **Surrender**. What we want - our own will - must be set aside if we truly desire God's direction. If we are yielded, we surrender ourselves and our own will. "I urge you therefore, brethren, by the mercies of God, to present your bodies a living and holy sacrifice, acceptable to God, which is your spiritual service of worship." Rom. 12:1 A yielding of the heart is an act of worship toward God.

PRINCIPLE: Our willingness to yield impacts our ability to hear.

If we want one thing, and God is trying to tell us another, then we keep questioning what God is speaking to us. We ask "Are you sure about that, Lord?" This "prayer" continues until we convince ourselves that God is saying what we want to hear.

Balaam was a very confused prophet. He was a man filled with greed. Balaam was hired to curse Israel for money, and he craved that money. Num. 22-24. But God wanted Balaam to bless Israel. Despite his best efforts to the contrary, Balaam could speak only what God told him. Balaam kept trying to curse Israel, but he could not. Balaam's employer, Balak, became a very frustrated man. "I called you to curse my enemies, but behold, you have persisted in blessing them these three times!" Num. 24:10.

Our **selfish motives** hinder our ability to hear God. If we persist in what we want, rather than completely surrendering to God, we show the spirit of Balaam and we will live in confusion. If we persist in the way that we think it should be, limited by a vision grounded by small faith, we can't perceive the depth of what God intends for our lives.

PRINCIPLE: What we want affects what we hear.

B. The second key is the **Presence and Work** of God around us. A Godly person is looking all around himself for the hand of God at work. "For I have taken all this to my heart and explain it that righteous men, wise men, and their deeds are in the hand of God." Ecc. 9:1. A righteous man is aware that God is at work in his life at all times - both in and around him.

How many times has God called precious saints to do the impossible? Yet when those saints take steps to obey God's direction, doors begin to open. Walls begin to fall. What doors around you are opening?

Isolation is a hindrance. It is a very dangerous place to be. Events and people around us are important indicators. If we tend to say we alone have the "word," we may only be shoring up our own insecurities, rather than serving God. Ecc. 4:8-12.

PRINCIPLE: A Godly person does not function in isolation.

C. A third key is **Discernment** between flesh and Spirit. "And do not be conformed to this world, but be transformed by the renewing of your mind, that you may prove what the will of God is, that which is good and acceptable and perfect." Rom. 12:2. We need to learn difference between our flesh and emotion (often a passing impulse) and the Spirit of God. The writer of

Hebrews admonishes us that "solid food is for the mature, who because of practice have their senses trained to discern good and evil." Heb. 5:14.

One of the most difficult areas of guidance is in affairs of the heart. How hard is it to discern whether that attractive person is the one intended for you? When you are in love, or have finally found some one who is special, how can you possibly set aside your feelings to discover the Lord's direction for you? In the discernment of age-old wisdom: "Marry in haste and repent at leisure."

Romance is one of the primary areas of deception for God's people, because it is so hard to put our personal feelings aside.

Our **Fleshly Impulses** can hinder our ability to hear a clear, pure Word. Each of us has "filters" that impact our ability to hear - our feelings, needs, personality, giftings, philosophies and dysfunctions. That is why fasting can be beneficial. It helps keep our flesh in check as we seek.

PRINCIPLE: Who we are can affect what we hear.

BUT realize that when some one senses a word, the fact it may be slanted or personalized does not mean God has not spoken to that person. Pastor Late has often admonished me: "Many times when some one speaks it is ten percent from God and ninety percent from man. Use discernment, but give some grace to your brother along with correction and acceptance."

D. The fourth key is the test of **scripture**. Revelation is always given in accordance with Scripture, and never contrary to it. "All scripture is inspired by God and profitable for teaching, for reproof, for correction, for training in righteousness; that the man of God may be adequate, equipped for every good work." II Tim. 3:16-17.

Literally, this verse says that scripture is "God-breathed." That "inspiration" applies both when the Word is given, and when the Word is received. We need both knowledge of scripture and illumination of it by the Holy Spirit. Cleopas and his friend knew scripture. They knew the law. They had religious heritage, background and traditions. But on the road to Emmaus, Jesus illuminated the scripture for them. "And beginning with Moses and with all the prophets, He explained to them the things concerning Himself in all the Scriptures." Lk. 24:27. As a result, their hearts came alive. "Were not our hearts **burning** within us while He was speaking to us on the road, while He was explaining the Scriptures to us?" Lk. 24:32.

PRINCIPLE: Scripture fights deception.

Titillation is a hindrance to revelation. Entertainment is a god of this generation. We seek the mind of the Lord, not just a word. Just a few verses after telling us that scripture is "God-inspired," Paul warns "For the time will come when they will not endure sound doctrine; but **wanting to have their ears tickled**, they will accumulate for themselves teachers in accordance with their own desires; and will turn away their ears from the truth, and will turn aside to myths." II Tim. 4:3-4. If what you hear tickles your fancy, beware.

E. The final key is **Peace**. Jesus promised the revelation of the Holy Spirit to His disciples. "But the Helper, the Holy Spirit, whom the Father will send in My name, **He will teach you all things**, and bring to your remembrance all that I said to you. Peace I leave you; My peace I give to you; not as the world gives, do I give to you. Let not your heart be troubled, nor let it be fearful." Jn. 14:26-27. Jesus promises revelation followed by a blessing of His peace. With His revelation, the Lord gives deep and abiding peace.

MEDITATION: "So then do not be foolish, but understand what the will of the Lord is." Eph. 5:17.

<u>QUESTIONS FOR GUIDANCE</u> (paraphrasing George Mueller*)

1. Have I yielded myself completely to God and His direction in this matter? Am I willing to obey any answer?

2. What is God doing around you?

3. Does the sensing persist or not? Is it a passing fancy or perhaps something more substantial?

4. What does scripture say about this matter?

5. Do you have peace in the matter, or is there confusion?

(*See *Financial Freedom*, Institute in Basic Youth Conflicts, p. 201)

REVIEW:
1. Through guidance, the Lord communicates His call.
2. God sends His people with direction.
3. The Lord gives perfect direction for His work.
4. Our willingness to yield impacts our ability to hear.
5. What we want affects what we hear.
6. A Godly person does not function in isolation.
7. Who we are can affect what we hear.
8. Revelation is always given in accordance with Scripture, and never contrary to it.
9. Scripture fights deception.
10. With His revelation, the Lord gives deep and abiding peace.

A REMINDER

On May 20, 2008 a little after 2:00 AM, I woke up. I prayed for a while. Then I pondered for a time. At 5:10 AM, I sensed something "click." It felt as if there was a release or a lifting of a burden or oppression. It did not impact me emotionally. But I sensed it in my spirit.

I went back to sleep and had the following dream:

I was attending a church meeting in a white, clapboard church. The congregation was my home church, but the sanctuary was completely different. High above the congregation was a small balcony with steep stairs on both sides that curved up from the sanctuary. I stood on the balcony in a line awaiting communion.

As I looked over the sanctuary below, white smoke began seeping under the doors and through the walls. The smoke was not gray or black like wood smoke. The windows of the church were covered on the inside with unpainted plywood. But the white smoke seeped around the plywood nonetheless.

The people of the congregation were concerned about the smoke and "buzzed," but no one panicked. I decided to forego communion, and check on the source of the white smoke.

I went down the balcony stairs and walked to the door at the front of the sanctuary. I paused before I opened the door, wondering if flames would be on the other side of it. But when I opened the door, the interior area beyond it also had seeping white smoke.

Puzzled, I went down another flight of stairs to the basement. Could it be the furnace? In the basement were double doors that led to a room which presumably housed the furnace. White smoke was billowing out of those doors and out of a vent into the finished basement beside the furnace room.

The basement was old. The atmosphere was a little dank, and the furnishings looked worn - as if the basement had been well used in the past, but not used recently. My attention was drawn to a wood table in the open room. On the table was a lamp and a porcelain tray. The tray had a rectangular shape and was curved up on each end. Its surface was enameled in an exquisite gold-lined design on a dark blue base.

74

The tray was empty, but out of the tray rose at least two columns of the white smoke. I leaned over to smell the white smoke from the tray. It was not acrid. The white smoke smelled like incense with a deep, sweet odor. "Ahhh!" I thought. "The presence of the Lord!" It was wonderful! I looked up from the tray and the double doors to the furnace room were gone. A smaller sealed panel was in their place. White smoke still billowed from the sealed panel.

I immediately wanted to tell the congregation so they could experience it, too. I bounded up the stairs shouting, "Taste and see! Taste and see! Taste and see that the Lord is good!"

Then I woke up.

Whether or not such dreams are "real" or from God, you can decide. But for me, this dream was a reminder. Revelation and guidance are essential to the life of the Christian disciple. That is why the first few chapters of this book focused on the impact of revelation. Revelation and guidance are keys to effective Christian ministry. We need them to understand and fulfill our call in Him. But the revelation of the Lord Himself is preeminent - and without comparison.

PRINCIPLE: The most precious revelation is the Lord Himself.

THE CYCLE OF DISCIPLESHIP

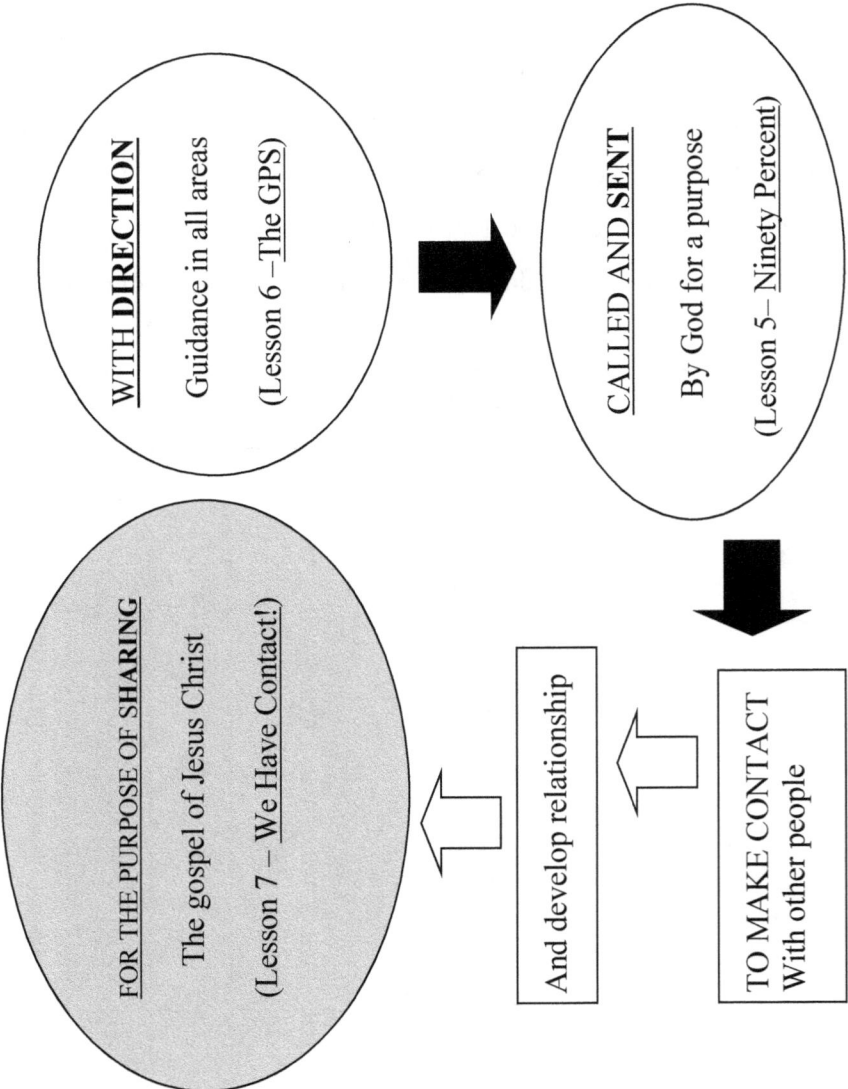

WITH DIRECTION

Guidance in all areas

(Lesson 6 – The GPS)

CALLED AND SENT

By God for a purpose

(Lesson 5– Ninety Percent)

FOR THE PURPOSE OF SHARING

The gospel of Jesus Christ

(Lesson 7 – We Have Contact!)

And develop relationship

TO MAKE CONTACT
With other people

THE CYCLE: SENT BY GOD WITH DIRECTION - **TO MAKE CONTACT FOR SHARING**

LESSON 7 - WE HAVE CONTACT!

I sat in a church in Durham, North Carolina. I had never been in that church before, and I never attended that church again. In fact, that church no longer exists. Yet as I sat in that church on that day, I felt my heart beat faster. My mind raced with excited thoughts. It seemed that a light had exploded within my whole being. At that point, I did not understand what "call" meant. Nonetheless, I was experiencing a call from the Lord.

I grew up loving football and basketball. I tried to play those sports - but was prevented from doing so because of injury and circumstance. I was an extremely disappointed young man. The sport I played in high school held no particular attraction for me initially. It was soccer. But I played soccer. It was a sport I could play with my injuries, and I loved to compete.

The summer before I went to that church in Durham, my church held a weekly Vacation Bible School for young children at a neighborhood apartment complex. Knowing the Bible called us to make disciples, I felt drawn to help. At the Vacation Bible School, the church workers held the Vacation Bible School with younger kids on one side of the field. But I observed a different dynamic on the other side of the field. There I saw an international mix of young men kicking a soccer ball around. It was unplanned, but I spent the rest my Vacation Bible School kicking a soccer ball with international teenagers and hanging out with them. Vacation Bible School ended, and I went back home.

A couple of weeks later I received a telephone call from a church friend. She heard that I had coached youth soccer, and she needed a soccer coach for a church recreation league team. I had coached recreation league soccer before. But I surveyed my life. I was working full time. I had a young family with two toddlers and another one on the way. I didn't believe I could spare the time. I called the friend back and said "No."

Then my family and I went to Durham to visit my sister. We rode the train from Charlotte to Durham for a friendly visit. On that Sunday, my sister and brother-in-law wanted to visit a "start up" church that was meeting in a hotel in Durham.

During the service, the pastor arose to speak. He previously was the pastor of one of the largest churches in Durham, but felt led to leave to start a new work. "I have a vision," the pastor announced. "I want this church to buy a large tract of land here near Durham."

I nestled down in my seat. "Here comes the building program!" I thought to myself.

"But," the pastor continued, "I don't want us to build church buildings there." I sat back up. "I want us to put ball fields on that land. Then, we are going to get some buses, back them up to the inner city in Durham, pick up kids and take them out to the fields that we have built. There those kids are going to play ball, and we are going to play with them. We are going to get to know them, relate to them, and share the gospel with them!"

At that moment, something clicked! It was as if a light bulb went on in my head. Soccer was a means of relationship. Through soccer, I could relate to the young international men. It was a means to make contact, to reach them and to influence them! My mind whirled with the possibilities.

But this moment was more than just a realization. My thoughts raced, and my heart beat faster. My hands trembled. If a siren had gone off beside me, it would not have made any more impact. The events of my younger life and the events of the last few months seemed to converge. Disparate and disjointed occurrences were woven into a meaningful tapestry. Circumstances in my life that previously baffled me now made sense. The Lord had been preparing me for this moment - for this call.

We rode the train back to Charlotte. I called my church friend and told her that I would coach the team under one condition - that I be allowed to include some international neighborhood children on the team. She was eager to find a coach, and had a couple of open spots for players on that team. That first season, I coached a team with two young Vietnamese boys on it - one boy with a Christian background, and one boy with a Buddhist background.

Thus came a call to ministry that is still ongoing as this story is written.

That flash of light - that dawning of revelation - changed my life. It was a defining moment for me. From that moment forward, my focus changed, my use of time changed, and my lifestyle changed. I felt as if God had given me a key. Although I did not realize the full impact at the time, my feelings were accurate. God had given me a key. That key was a means to establish relationship with the persons to whom God had sent me. God had shown me how to make contact.

PRINCIPLE: Through call, God sends us to make contact with people.

MAKING CONTACT

When I was participating in the Vacation Bible School, I was actually drawn to a group that was not a part of the Vacation Bible School - a group of refugee young men. The Lord was birthing a call in my life to that group of people. But I had a problem. I did not know how to make contact with that group of young men. I did not know how to enter their lives.

Through that epiphany in that church in Durham, NC, I realized the means to make contact with the group to which I was called. Soccer was a means to impact the lives of young men. Yet soccer is only one of thousands of ways to make contact. Contact can be made through music, art, meeting a need, education, camping, biking, surfing, etc. The list is as long as the list of human activities and endeavors.

One day I arrived at a new soccer venue to find our soccer goals missing. I called the field supervisor, but there was no clue of their whereabouts. After a search of the surrounding area, we found the goals in the back yard of a neighboring house. As my players and I began to retrieve the goals, a teenager emerged from the house and asked, "What are doing with our goals?"

"These are our goals" I responded.

"My dad paid a man $50.00 for these goals," the teenager argued. "A man drove up with them in the back of his truck and sold them to us."

More teenagers came out of neighboring houses. I sensed an impending confrontation. I pointed out a couple of distinctive markers on the goals that demonstrated

our ownership.

Then I had an idea. These young men obviously loved soccer. "Listen" I said, "we need to move these goals back to the field. But why don't you and your friends come play soccer with us?"

And they did - week after week. Thus, we made contact with Noah (the teenager), and three other neighborhood young men, as a result of two stolen soccer goals.

PRINCIPLE: God shows us how to make contact.

THE PURPOSE OF CONTACT

What is the purpose of contact? God sends us to make contact in order to establish His Kingship in the lives of others. We make contact so we initially can share about Him and His kingdom. When Jesus sent His disciples, He instructed them about the purpose of the mission. "And as you go, preach, saying, 'The kingdom of heaven is at hand." Mt. 10:7.

Paul understood this purpose. "But when He who had set me apart, even from my mother's womb, and called me through His grace, was pleased to reveal His Son in me, that I might preach Him among the Gentiles..." Gal. 1:15-16. Paul understood that the purpose of His call was to proclaim the Gospel to those persons to whom he was sent.

Likewise, Paul urged Timothy to share the Gospel. "But you, be sober in all things, endure hardship, do the work of an evangelist, fulfill your ministry." II Tim. 4:5.

PRINCIPLE: God sends us to make contact for the purpose of sharing the Gospel.

After I experienced a call, the first soccer season ended. I went home and the players went home. That winter, I knocked on doors and visited refugee families that had just arrived in America. One of my young refugee players, Van, went with me on some of those visits and helped to translate for some of the new families.

The next soccer season, I had four refugee young men playing on my team. We had a great season. As we rode home from the last game, one of the young men spoke up. "Coach, are we going to play next week?"

I was tired. "The season is over. We are going home. We'll play again next year."

"But coach, we want to keep playing soccer."

I shook my head. "The season is over. We don't have any more games."

"But coach, we can keep playing."

I continued to make rational objections. "There are only four of you. That isn't enough people to play a soccer game."

"We have friends that want to play. We can bring our friends."

I paused for a minute. Was God doing something here? We did have a very small field at the church. Also, I really liked these guys. I hated to end our relationship.

"I tell you what," I said. "Next Sunday afternoon, I will be at the field at the church at three o'clock. If you guys want to play, bring your friends and we will play soccer."

I didn't know what to expect. But I showed up the next Sunday at the field. And so did they - with plenty of friends. In the following weeks, they brought friends, who brought friends, who brought friends.

Thus began Sunday afternoon soccer. Weekly soccer on Sunday that went on for 15 years in which hundreds of young men participated. It was a time of fun, interaction, and sharing. I would like to say that it was my idea - but that would not really be truthful.

I learned something from that experience.

First, friends bring friends. Once I made contact with just a couple of young men, I didn't need to do much more promotion. The young men brought their friends. Jesus made contact with one woman at a well in John 4. She then brought a whole city to Him, causing Him to say, "Behold, I say to you, lift up your eyes, and look on the fields, that they are white for harvest." Jn. 4:28-30, 35.

PRINCIPLE: After we make contact, friends bring friends.

81

Second, I had built a relationship with those young men through a season of coaching. They hated, and I hated, to see that relationship end.

EFFECTIVE SHARING

Advir loved to come to soccer camp. At first I found this attraction strange. Advir did not play soccer. At soccer camp, Advir hung around the edge of the field while the other campers played. He helped with occasional tasks, but he didn't participate in the drills, in the fun competitions, or in the soccer games. "Most unusual," I thought to myself, "that a young man wants to attend soccer camp when he doesn't appear to have any interest in the game of soccer." But year after year, Advir would be there when we picked the guys up for camp.

I did notice that Advir loved to ride in the front passenger seat of the van that I drove. Every time we rode to the camp and every time we rode back from the camp, Advir was the first person in the van - eagerly claiming his spot in the front seat. As we rode, Advir and I talked. I heard about his background - how he grew up in war torn Bosnia. I heard about the trauma of war - how war had ravaged his hometown and how many people in his village had died, including some of Advir's own family members. I heard about the flight of his family and about the harrowing life of a refugee. Advir also told me that he struggled with his self control. But he was attending classes to help with his temper and he was trying to learn to control it. I encouraged Advir in that struggle, and received regular updates about it.

Eventually, I concluded that Advir didn't come to camp to play soccer. He came to camp because it was an opportunity to converse - an opportunity to relate. Through the years, I realized that some of my best interactions came from riding in the van - riding to camps, riding to practices, riding to games, and riding to retreats.

Riding in the van, I heard Li Chung's story. Li fled Vietnam tightly packed in a little boat with scores of other refugees. Other family members, including Li's brother, rode in another boat beside them. But a fierce storm arose in the China Sea. Li watched in horror as his brother's boat capsized in the raging sea and all of its passengers, including his brother, drowned. Then Li spent seven years in a refugee camp near Hong Kong until he could come to the United States.

Riding in the van, I heard Mohamed Shareef's story. Mohamed lived in Somalia - a country caught in the grip of an awful civil war. Mohamed had a sister who was six years older than Mohamed. One day rebels came to Mohamed's village - intent on mayhem. Mohamed and his family hid for safety. But the rebels caught his sister, and as a six year old boy, Mohamed watched as his sister was shot and killed.

Riding in the van is where Mahir told me that his forehead was "like a rock." Riding in the van is where Van told me he was so nervous that he could "barely stand it." Riding in the van, I heard about families, about schools, about hopes, about dreams and about beliefs. Riding in the van I heard about tragedies; I shared in laughter; and I spoke to the hearts of young men. Through the years, some of the most important discussions - some of the most meaningful interactions - occurred while riding in the van.

Relationship is a key to effective gospel sharing. In a good relationship, trust is built and love is shared. When you invest the time necessary to develop trust and to share love, then you build a platform from which to share - a platform of credibility. It is a platform from which you can speak Words of life into the heart of another human.

PRINCIPLE: Influential sharing arises out of relationship.

THE IMPORTANCE OF RELATIONSHIP

Jesus emphasized the effectiveness of relational sharing in both His instructions and His actions. Study carefully Jesus' instructions to the seventy followers that He sent out in Luke 10. "And whatever house you enter, first say 'Peace be to this house.'" Lk. 10:5. Jesus didn't just send the disciples to cities. He sent them to homes.

"And stay in that house, eating and drinking what they give you; for the laborer is worthy of his wages. *Do not keep moving from house to house.*" Lk. 10:7. To stay in many homes during an outreach touches more people. To stay in one home during the outreach builds deeper relationship with the persons in that home. Jesus' instructions emphasized depth of contact as much or more than the number of contacts.

PRINCIPLE: In the kingdom of God, the quality of sharing is measured by depth.

"And stay in that house, eating and drinking what they give you; for the laborer is worthy of his wages. Do not keep moving from house to house. And in whatever city you enter, and they receive you, eat what is set before you..." Lk. 10:7-8. Eating together is a great way of sharing. Breaking bread in peace helps to break down barriers. Breaking bread in fellowship encourages sharing from the heart. I search for opportunities to eat together so sharing can flow.

My friend, Barney, and I took a group of Montegnard young men on a mountain retreat. The Montegnard people lived in the mountains of Vietnam. They were harshly persecuted by the communist government for years after the Vietnam War because they assisted the United States in the Vietnam war, and because the Montegnard people were a different ethnicity than most Vietnamese. Barney and I were trying to build a relationship with these young refugees. One purpose of our mountain retreat was to introduce the young men to the North Carolina mountains. I, however, was the one about to receive a cultural education.

For supper on the road, I chose Cracker Barrel. I was certain that Cracker Barrel had something that everyone could eat, and besides, I loved Cracker Barrel. The menu had chicken on it and chicken is what most of the Montegnard young men chose. We had to pick sides to go with the chicken. For visual appeal, the menu showed a beautiful, ripe fresh apple. Each of our guests pointed excitedly to the apple. We ordered apples for every one of them. When the sides were served, though, they weren't fresh apples. They were delicious, baked cinnamon apples. Delicious to me, that is. The young men tasted them and did not like them. To my consternation, when we left the restaurant that evening, there were seven

dishes of apples sitting on the table - uneaten.

Determined to defer to our guests, Barney and I took them to the grocery store to shop for breakfast the next morning. I showed the guys what Americans typically had for breakfast - and received the same response for each item.

"This is what we call breakfast cereal. We eat it with milk. Do you like cereal and milk?"

"No."

"This is bacon. We can have bacon, eggs and biscuits. Do you like bacon?"

"No."

"Here is oatmeal. It is a hot cereal that you serve with sugar and milk. Do you like oatmeal?"

"No."

"Here are pop tarts with fruit in them. They are sweet and taste good. Do you like pop tarts?"

"No."

Barney and I ultimately purchased what our guests liked, but I was shaking my head as I left the grocery store. For breakfast the next morning we fixed rice, meatballs, and toast, served with hot sauce, and, of course, fresh apples. It actually was a pretty good breakfast.

"Eating what is set before you" is a means of bridging what divides. It is entering into the culture of your call. Eating what is set before you demonstrates that your host's culture - his paradigm - is meaningful to you. It allows your host to share with you, and creates an atmosphere conducive to you sharing with him.

How interesting that Jesus' instructions to His disciples included details of dining! Jesus, of course, did not teach a relational method of sharing without demonstrating it Himself. By His own description, He came "eating and drinking." Lk. 7:34. Consider the number of people with whom Jesus "hung out." Jesus spent large amounts of time with His twelve disciples, pouring His heart into them. After all, the Twelve were those that the Father had "given" Him. Jn. 17:12. In addition to the twelve disciples, though, Jesus socialized with Simon the Pharisee (Lk. 7:40);

Zaccheus (Lk. 19:5); unnamed Pharisees (Lk. 11:37 and 14:1); Lazarus, Mary and Martha (Jn. 12:2); numerous publicans with Levi (Lk. 5:29); and the people of a Samaritan village (Jn. 4:40).

PRINCIPLE: Influence occurs when you enter the world of the other person.

MEDITATION: "For He whom God has sent speaks the words of God; for He gives the Spirit without measure." Jn. 3:34.

1. What is the correlation between speaking words of God and the Holy Spirit?

2. For what purpose did God give His Spirit to the church? See Jn. 15:26-27; Acts 1:8.

3. What methods has the Lord shown you to make contact with other people?

4. How do you feel about sharing the gospel with those around you?

5. Here is a quote attributed to St. Francis of Assisi: "Preach the gospel constantly and, if necessary, use words." Which is the more effective method of sharing - preaching or dining?

REVIEW:

1. Through call, God sends us to make contact with people.
2. God shows us how to make contact.
3. God sends us to make contact for the purpose of sharing the Gospel.
4. After we make contact, friends bring friends.
5. Influential sharing arises out of relationship.
6. In the kingdom of God, the quality of sharing is measured by depth.
7. Influence occurs when you enter the world of the other person.

THE CYCLE OF DISCIPLESHIP

FOR THE PURPOSE OF CARING

And helping others to heal and to grow

(Lesson 8 – But Coach, It's Like Family!)

WITH DIRECTION

Guidance in all areas

(Lesson 6 –The GPS)

CALLED AND SENT

By God for a purpose

(Lesson 5– Ninety Percent)

FOR THE PURPOSE OF SHARING

The gospel of Jesus Christ

(Lesson 7 – We Have Contact!)

And develop relationship

TO MAKE CONTACT
With other people

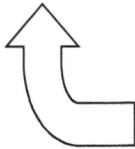

88

LESSON 8 - "BUT COACH, IT'S LIKE FAMILY!"

Victor was a young man from Serbia. I met Victor when he was seven years old. Victor was too young to play soccer with us on Sundays, but he still showed up and hung around the field. Victor kind of floated in and out of the area over the course of the afternoon. As I watched him, the word "waif" came to mind.

One thing that I began to notice is that Victor always had some type of wound or injury. He had a large, multi-colored bruise on his leg; or a deep gash on his back; or a cast on his arm due to a broken bone. Victor was very energetic and precocious. He was unkempt and very thin. Victor referred to himself as "Mr. Skinny."

I surmised that Victor did not receive much supervision at home. In my discussions with him, he confirmed that he was left on his own during the day, roaming a neighborhood rife with crime, drugs, and gangs. I shuddered to think of the dangers for a seven year old boy in that area. Indeed, many of the inner city children had little supervision. Some parents didn't care. Other parents cared, but they had to work two or three jobs to make ends meet. They didn't have a choice.

Victor's behavior struck me as strange. When other children brought bicycles to the soccer field, Victor borrowed one. I had a longstanding rule that no bicycles were allowed on the field. What little grass remained on that bedraggled and overused pitch did not need to be subjected to bicycle tires in addition to the scores of cleats, tennis shoes and bare feet of the players. Victor, however, routinely rode a bicycle onto the field. He didn't really seem to mind it when I upbraided him. In fact no matter how strongly I had chastised him before, the next week here came Victor again, riding a bicycle across the field right in front of me. It was perplexing behavior.

When Victor grew big enough to start playing soccer with us, he was enthusiastic and personable. I observed that when his good behavior resulted in attention, he behaved well. If that attention waned, however, Victor would begin to misbehave. He endured the discipline for his misbehavior, and then a few minutes later, repeated the same misbehavior. Oddly enough, when you scolded him, his facial expression almost reflected pleasure. That dynamic puzzled me for months.

What I eventually concluded is that, for Victor, as well as for many other young men, it was not a matter of good attention or bad attention. It was simply a matter of attention. Any attention, even negative attention, was good attention. These young men did not receive much attention at home and so they did whatever it took to attract attention to themselves on the soccer field or off.

Watching young people can tell you a lot. You watch them play or interact with their peers. Some children are obviously thriving. They are secure in their boundaries and at peace with other people and with themselves. Other children are disjointed. Their actions are inconsistent. One minute they seem engaged; but the next minute they disconnect. The needs that we found in our ministry were incredible.

I learned something else through the years. On the soccer field, I wasn't the only one observing. As I was watching them, the children were watching me. Children understand the motivation of persons around them. Children understand when they are being loved. They also sense when the interaction has a different motivation.

My friend, Goose, was employed by a local church. The church paid for Goose to travel to Los Angeles and spend a week observing a reputable inner city ministry. When Goose came back, he seemed a little shaken. I asked Goose what happened.

He said, "One day I went with a team to pass out food and water to some homeless guys. We drove down to a shelter that had tons of homeless people. The ministry guys passing out the supplies were a little brusque. They were focused on crowd control, and spoke sternly to a number of the homeless men gathered to receive food. I went and stood in the line with the homeless men to talk to them and to help facilitate the distribution.

"When I was standing in the line, one of the homeless men asked me why I was there. I told him it was because I cared about them. He looked me in the eye, and then he said this: 'If you really cared about us, you would live your life differently.' I just can't shake what he said, because he was right. If I really cared about them, I would go be with them and spend time with them - not just go pass out food."

When we try to "minister" to a person or a group of people, we usually have an agenda. That agenda may be a very positive one. We may want to convert them with the Gospel, or to ask them to join our church. But their perspective is based on an overriding need that we all have. And they quickly discern your motivation. They want to know - DO YOU LOVE THEM? Do you really care for them? Do you have the heart of a shepherd?

"For God so loved the world that He gave His only begotten Son..." Jn. 3:16. God sent Jesus into the world as a manifestation of His love. When God sends us, it is the same. We show a manifestation of the love of God to the world - an extension of God's love to those persons to whom God sends us.

> PRINCIPLE: When God calls a person, He gives that person love for the people to whom he is called.

WHY IS A SHEPHERD A SHEPHERD?

One time I read a scripture that struck me as odd. In Matthew 9, Jesus felt compassion for the multitudes "because they were distressed and downcast like sheep without a shepherd." Mt. 9:36. Then Jesus turned to His disciples and exhorted them. "The harvest is plentiful, but the workers are few. Therefore beseech the Lord of the harvest to send out workers into His harvest." Mt. 9:37-38.

"Most unusual," I thought. "A shepherd cares for his flock. Jesus is in a shepherding mode, but immediately directs attention to persons who are outside of the flock. Why is this?"

Pastor Late was a wise and insightful man. The next time I met with him, I brought up this passage and expressed my puzzlement. I said, "This passage has a disconnect. Jesus had His flock around Him. Why would Jesus direct His feelings as a Shepherd to those who were unsaved - to those outside of the flock, instead of the ones in His flock?"

Pastor Late paused for a minute and then asked, "Why is a shepherd a shepherd?"

"I don't know," I lamely responded. "Why is a shepherd a shepherd?"

Pastor Late said "A shepherd is a shepherd because a shepherd loves sheep. It doesn't matter whether the sheep are in his flock or outside of his flock. A shepherd loves sheep."

When the Lord calls a person to reach others, that person becomes a shepherd in the circles in which he walks. A shepherd cares for the sheep around him. He nurtures, feeds, protects, and heals them. The shepherd's work flows naturally from the love and concern that he has for sheep. In the areas of my life that I operate - family, work, church, and outreach - I see myself as a shepherd. It is simple care for another person.

> PRINCIPLE: God sends us to care for people.

THE WHOLE PERSON

Abdulahi was a good player. He had played on a couple of our teams. We were in the middle of a soccer season.

Yosef had tried out for the team, but he didn't make the cut. Still, he came to some of our practices. He didn't come so much to play soccer as to be around the team. Yosef hung around the fringes while we ran our drills, and then interacted with me and the guys during the breaks.

One day, Abdulahi came to practice in his street clothes. "Where is your gear?" I asked.

Abdulahi held up his hand. The whole hand was heavily bandaged and he had a splint on his finger. "Abdulahi!" I exclaimed. "What happened?"

Abdulahi looked embarrassed. "I hurt my finger, Coach."

Another player spoke up. "He got in a fight, Coach."

"Adbulahi, tell me how you hurt your finger!" I demanded.

"It was Yosef, Coach. I got in a fight with Yosef and he bit my finger. I can't play, Coach."

The other player chimed in. "Yosef just about bit his finger off. Abdulahi had to go to the hospital."

"How long are you going to be out?" I asked.

"The doctor said I can't play for three or four weeks."

Abdulahi showed up for the next practice in his street clothes. Yosef was nowhere to be seen. We went through the practice with Abdulahi watching from the sidelines.

After the practice, Abdulahi came over to see me. "I have a question, Coach." he said.

"What is it, Abdulahi?"

"It's about Yosef, Coach. Since I'm not going to be playing for a few weeks, I was wondering - well - if Yosef could take my place on the team."

I stopped for a moment - not sure that I had heard correctly. "You want Yosef to take your place on the team?" I asked incredulously.

"Yeah, Coach. You know - since I can't play."

"Abdulahi, I thought Yosef was the guy that just about bit your finger off!"

"He did, Coach."

"How can you want the guy that injured you to take your place?"

Abdulahi paused and shrugged his shoulders. "He's my friend, Coach."

I left practice that day shaking my head. What a culture!

Yosef did not play on the team that season. A few months later, the guys told me that Yosef was in the hospital. He had experienced severe stomach pain and had surgery on his abdomen.

The next day was a very busy day at work. During lunchtime, though, I slipped out and went over to the hospital to see Yosef. I knocked on the door of Yosef's hospital room and he was awake.

As I entered the room, I realized it was the most empty hospital room I have ever seen - no people, no flowers, and no pictures. It was just Yosef in a hospital bed alone with

white walls and white sheets. He seemed pleased to see me.

I talked with Yosef awhile, shared with him, and then left. The visit was not very convenient, but as I walked out of the hospital, I was glad that I went.

Effective ministry addresses the needs of the whole person - physical, emotional, intellectual and spiritual. Jesus understood this dynamic. When He sent His twelve disciples, Jesus told them to proclaim the Kingdom. But Jesus did not just tell them to proclaim the kingdom. Jesus also said, "Heal the sick, raise the dead, cleanse the lepers, cast out demons; freely you received, freely give." Mt. 10:8. Jesus instructed His disciples to meet the needs of the persons to whom they ministered - to care for the whole person.

PRINCIPLE: The needs of the whole person are important.

My ministry partner, Goose, teaches me a lot about ministry. One wonderful thing I observed about Goose is that he tries to meet the needs of the people around him. When Goose sees a need, he immediately sets out to resolve it.

One day, Goose visited a poor Somali family with a Muslim background. The family of eight lived in a small, two-bedroom apartment. As Goose talked with the father, cockroaches were crawling in and out of the beds. Goose realized that the family's wooden bed frames were cockroach infested.

Within a couple of days, Goose had located some bunkbeds from a camp. He rented a U-Haul truck. With the help of some of his soccer players, he delivered new beds to the family and removed the old infested ones.

Through the years, my coworkers and I have developed other means besides soccer to meet the needs of the youth to whom we ministered. We held summer day camps, weekend soccer camps, block parties, and weekend mountain retreats. We offered tutoring, life skills training, functional arts, and teaching.

God called His people to meet all needs of the person. Our care for people demonstrates our faith and our love. "If a brother or sister is without clothing and in need of daily food, and one of you says to them, 'Go in peace, be warmed and be filled,' and yet you do not give them what is necessary for their body, what use is that?" Jm. 2:15-16.

PRINCIPLE: The gospel is not shared in word only.

WHO WILL RESPOND?

I have a prayer list. I pray that list often, but I am convicted that I do not pray that list as often as I should.

On that list is the name of every young person that participated in our soccer outreach. Many on that list are still around, and many are long gone. But my prayers for all of them continue.

It is sometimes a sad process. It is sad, but it is scriptural. God sends us to share, and God sends us to care. At some point, though, we need to discern who is responding to the gospel. In whose heart is the Holy Spirit working?

How do we discern who is responding to the Gospel? It isn't just those persons who make a confession of faith or those persons who say they believe. It is those persons who repent. The hallmark of repentance is change. It is those persons whose faith results in change in their life.

The ministry of John the Baptist focused on repentance. "John baptized with the baptism of repentance." Acts 19:4a. But John wasn't just looking for a confession of repentance and baptism. He exhorted his hearers, "Therefore bring forth fruits in keeping with your repentance..." Lk. 3:8a. John preached repentance that resulted in meaningful change. The proof is in the pudding.

The persons that respond are those who change. They are the ones in whom repentance produces fruit. They are the ones on whom we need to focus our efforts.

When we discern a positive response confirmed by change, then we need to focus special attention on that person. It is not that we exclude others or that we stop sharing and reaching out to the world. When a person responds to the Gospel, though, God calls us to disciple that person - to help him grow and to help him mature. God calls us to shepherd him.

It is not that I have given up on the others. I continue to care for them and to pray for them. But I am focused on the faithful because those persons are moving further along the cycle of discipleship and have the possibility of completing it.

Nonetheless, the process has an element of sadness as you realize that more time spent with those persons who do respond means less time spent with those that do not.

Looking at him, Jesus felt a love for him and said to him, "One thing you lack; go and sell all you possess and give to the poor, and you will have treasure in heaven; and come, follow Me." But at these words he was saddened, and he went away grieving, for he was one that owned much property. Mk. 10:21-22.

PRINCIPLE: A good shepherd makes disciples of Jesus.

After I had coached soccer teams for a few years, I invited my players to come to my house for a weekly Bible study. A Bible study had been on my heart for a number of years. A few of my players responded. But after the players started coming, the study lasted for years.

One night, Chad, a young Liberian, visited our study. He raised his hand and asked a question. "You guys know that coach has been our soccer coach for a while. I was just wondering how coach has influenced you. Is there anything that impacted you?"

Kennedy raised his hand. "The first year that I played for coach, I struggled. I wasn't a very good player yet, but coach kept encouraging me and I kept trying. At one point coach said to me, 'Kennedy, you have the heart of a lion.' I didn't understand what he was talking about, but later on I realized he was right. I had it in my heart that I was going to make the team, and I didn't give up."

Next, Jorge spoke up. "When I played for coach, he encouraged me too. One time he told me, 'Jorge, you are a leader.' I didn't believe him when he said that. I was only a ninth grader then. A couple of years later, a teacher told me the same thing in class. I thought back to what coach had said and decided he was right. Now I believe I am a leader."

Nifa raised his hand. "Coach told me that I was quiet but deep - like deep water. It made me more comfortable because that is how God made me."

I was appreciative of the sharing by the guys. But what struck me was that each person shared was something that I had said that was specific to that person. Influence occurred because I pursued a deeper relationship with each person and was thus able to speak something into that person's life.

Part of the responsibility of call is responsibility for the people to whom God calls you. Conversion of a person is not the end of a ministry. It is only the beginning of discipleship.

God calls His people to run the race to the finish line. I Cor. 9:24. Sometimes, though, we mistake the starting block for the finish line. We start a person on the race, and then abandon him. Making disciples as the Lord instructed us implies that we help others complete the cycle of discipleship.

We can not discern the response to the Gospel or real change in the life of the disciple unless we spend time with that person. Discipleship requires time and attention. Only through close relationship can we begin to sense that change, and then help that person grow in his faith and relationship with the Lord.

PRINCIPLE: Care for a person means that you do not abandon him in his walk.

One season I did not have a team. I had coached a soccer team each fall for a number of years. But one fall the string stopped. Scheduling games was difficult. Some players graduated and others dropped out of school. I tried to salvage the season, but I failed. I was very tired.

Tom had played for me for three years. He was entering his senior year of high school and wanted to play. I felt the obligation to tell each player personally that the season was canceled.

I approached Tom and tried to explain the situation. I gave him all the excuses. We didn't have a full schedule. We were short a few players.

Tom shook his head. "Coach, I want to play."

"I know Tom and I really appreciate it. You have been a wonderful player and a good teammate. But I just don't feel we can pull it off this year."

Then, Tom said something that was bittersweet. It was affirming, but at the same time it was painful for me to hear. "But Coach!" he protested. "Coach...it's like family!"

MEDITATION: "But I hope in the Lord Jesus to send Timothy to you shortly, so that I also may be encouraged when I learn of your condition. For I have no one else of kindred spirit who will genuinely be concerned for your welfare." Phil. 2:19-20.

1. Do you sense the personal concern that Paul had for the Philippians?

2. Do you consider yourself as a shepherd in any venues such as work, home, neighborhood, club or church?

3. If so, how do you care for the people around you?

4. Why are the needs of the whole person important?

5. To what extent should our ministry focus "narrow" to persons who respond to the gospel?

REVIEW:

1. When God calls a person, He gives that person love for the people to whom he is called.
2. God sends us to care for people.
3. The needs of the whole person are important.
4. Effective ministry addresses the needs of the whole person.
5. The gospel is not shared in word only.
6. A good shepherd makes disciples of Jesus.
7. Care for a person means that you do not abandon him in his walk.

THE CYCLE OF DISCIPLESHIP

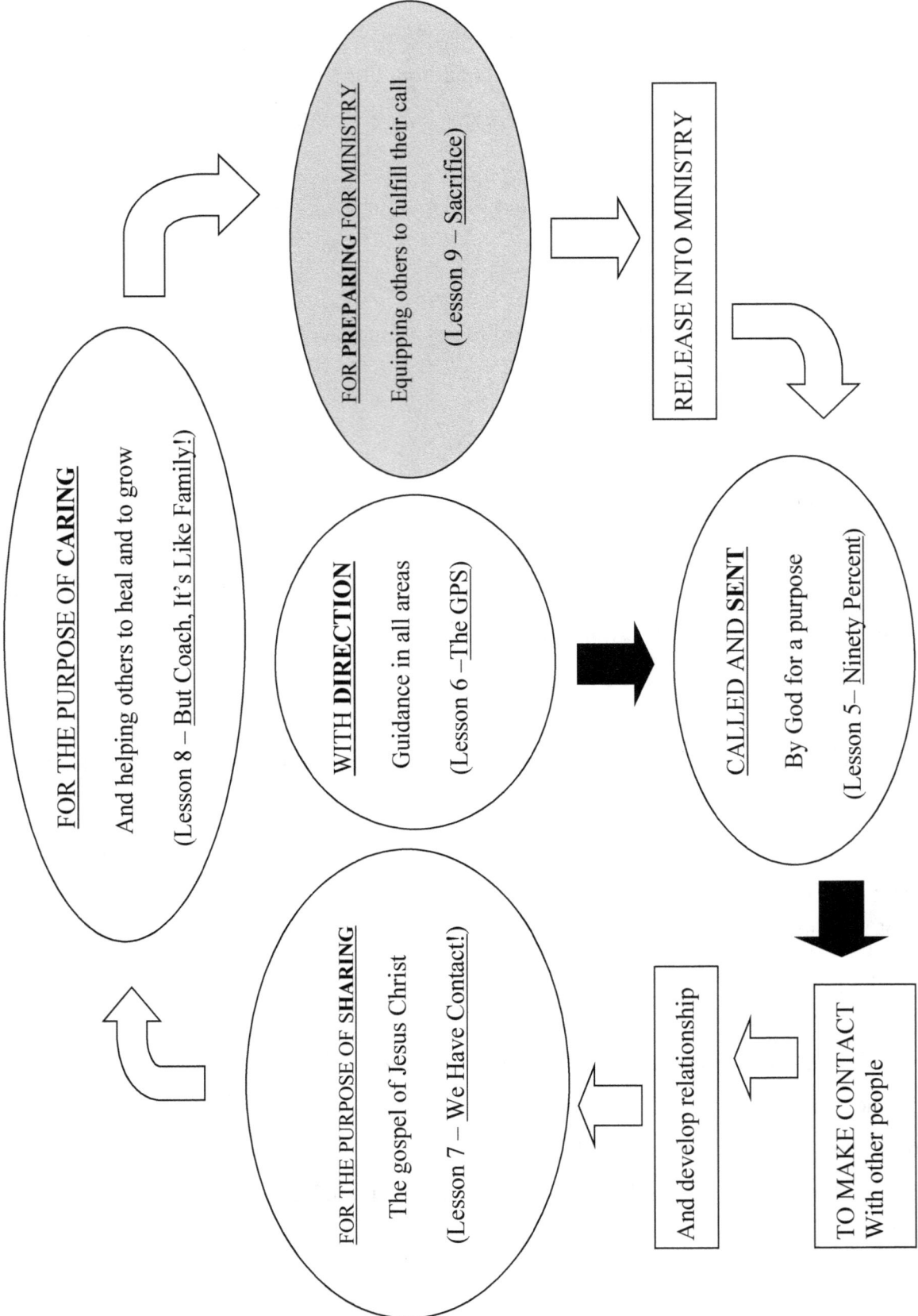

FOR **PREPARING** FOR MINISTRY

Equipping others to fulfill their call

(Lesson 9 – Sacrifice)

RELEASE INTO MINISTRY

FOR THE PURPOSE OF CARING

And helping others to heal and to grow

(Lesson 8 – But Coach, It's Like Family!)

WITH **DIRECTION**

Guidance in all areas

(Lesson 6 – The GPS)

CALLED AND **SENT**

By God for a purpose

(Lesson 5 – Ninety Percent)

FOR THE PURPOSE OF **SHARING**

The gospel of Jesus Christ

(Lesson 7 – We Have Contact!)

And develop relationship

TO MAKE CONTACT
With other people

THE CYCLE: SENT BY GOD WITH DIRECTION **- TO MAKE CONTACT** FOR SHARING, FOR CARING, AND **FOR PREPARING OTHERS FOR MINISTRY**

LESSON 9 - SACRIFICE

Parenting is at the same time both delightful and difficult. When children are young, good parents surround them with close guidance and protection. The teenage years, however, present different challenges. Parents have the job of loving their teenage children, but simultaneously preparing them for life on their own as adults.

My sixteen year old daughter obtained her driver's license. She wanted to drive to a friend's house alone after dark. My wife and I discussed whether she should be allowed to make this trip, and discovered that we had differing opinions.

My wife was concerned for our daughter's safety. Our daughter did not have much experience driving - much less driving after dark. My wife was concerned that she might have an accident, or that the car might break down and our daughter find herself stranded alone in the dark.

My perspective was that our daughter needed to learn to drive a car. The best training for driving was by doing it. Furthermore, our daughter needed to learn to fend for herself. She was in eleventh grade. In a short time she would be living at college - on her own and making decisions without us. She needed practice.

Fundamentally, my wife and I approached this issue from two different perspectives. My wife had the perspective of a shepherd. She concerned herself with the safety and welfare of our daughter. Thus, she wanted to smother her with care.

I had the perspective of a teacher. I wanted my daughter to learn and to grow to maturity so she could function on her own. I was willing to allow more risks in order to teach my daughter driving and good decision making.

When God calls us and sends us, it is vital to realize the purpose of that call. God calls us to proclaim, to convert and to shepherd. Many times, though, we are content if the persons to whom we are called remain as sheep. If they join our church and become members of "our

101

flock," that is sufficient. We then smother them with care (or not).

At that point though, the purpose of our call is not complete. God also calls us to prepare those persons for ministry. They themselves need to be called and sent by God. Our work is unfulfilled until those disciples are mature and equipped to minister on their own. Every disciple should be fruit-bearing. "By this is My Father glorified, that you bear much fruit, and *so prove* to be My disciples." Jn. 15:8. The proof is in the pudding. Disciples need to complete the cycle of discipleship.

> PRINCIPLE: God calls us to make disciples who make disciples.

CULTIVATING A CALL

Through the years at Boyz Club, we have always searched for leaders - leaders to help; leaders to participate in the work; and leaders to replicate and improve that area of ministry.

Many potential leaders have come to "check out" Boyz Club. Reactions vary. Here is a common reaction: "I love what you guys are doing here. This is super! You guys are building in the lives of these young men. I think God is calling me to help here. I will definitely be here next week. You can count on it!"

Then, we never see that person again.

Others have come back. Some have stayed for a few weeks; some for months or for years. Some are still there. These are ones who "stick." They feel called to the work, and have been living out that call as they have been given the grace to do so.

My encouragement to potential leaders is the same. "Do what the Lord has called you to do." If they do not come back, I don't fret.

Where does call originate? It is birthed in the heart of the disciple. Other believers may help discern that call. Other believers may encourage that call or they may help develop it. But the called disciple must have the call within them so that they have the foundation in their heart necessary to fulfill it.

Sometimes, we have the expectation that everyone should join our work. They are our "assistants" participating in our paradigm under our direction. My expectation is for every believer to hear from God for himself. If that call leads to a partnership in ministry, I rejoice. If not, I trust the Lord and rejoice anyway.

PRINCIPLE: Call dwells in the heart of the disciple.

SIDE BY SIDE

At my Bible study, I had a group of young men that I was trying to help disciple. We met weekly and enjoyed the time together. One week we decided to go to a Christian concert featuring some quality groups.

But there was a problem. The concert had been hastily arranged. When we arrived at the venue parking lot, it was almost empty. We saw a van that might belong to the tour singers, and a couple of other cars. But that was it. Maybe we had come to the wrong place. We were unsure whether even to go in.

We did go in, though, and we had come to the right place. The bands had set up all their equipment. My little group of five young men was half the audience. The rest were ministry organizers.

Before the concert began, I walked over to speak to one of the organizers. "You know," I said, "long ago I learned not to focus on numbers. I have been to outreaches where large numbers of young men came, and it has been mass chaos. Meaningful relationship with any of them was impossible.

"Likewise, I have been to outreach events with only four or five in attendance. Those times seemed richer and deeper. I related to them more intimately and dearly. Numbers can be an indicator, but they don't really measure meaningful ministry."

The organizer nodded her head and agreed. "Some of my best ministry has been to small groups," she said.

To their credit, the tour groups performed that evening with energy and feeling as if they had an audience of hundreds. Perhaps more importantly, after the concert, they came and mingled with the young people, talking with and ministering to them one on one.

I don't think the young men with me will ever forget that concert. They were thrilled.

How do we help encourage and develop the call of another disciple? Through an intimate relationship with that person. We must discern the heart.

Effective training requires a deeper sacrifice than public ministry. The teacher lays aside "ministry success" as measured in numbers in order to build individual skill. Public glory gives way to nurturing private growth. Through this private growth, the disciple becomes a leader, and not just a follower. The disciple matures into ministry.

Think of Jesus and His twelve disciples. Sometimes, even twelve was too many, and Jesus took aside fewer - like Peter, James and John - in order to prepare them for ministry. Effective preparation requires small numbers - often just two people ministering together alone.

A sacrifice of preparation is the sacrifice of time and attention. Paul was willing to put in this time. He reminded the elders at Ephesus "You yourselves know, from the first day that I set foot in Asia, how I was with you the whole time...therefore be on the alert, remembering that night and day *for a period of three years* I did not cease to admonish each one with tears..." Acts 20:18, 31.

PRINCIPLE: Preparing a disciple for ministry requires individual attention.

STEP BY STEP

When we bought my daughter a bicycle, she wanted to learn to ride it. I instructed her on the operation of a bicycle and demonstrated to her how to do it. But she needed to

104

try it on her own in order to learn how to ride. At some point, I had to get off the bicycle and let her get on.

After some near accidents and some actual spills, my daughter learned how to ride. We took a walk one day. I was on foot, and my daughter on her bike. We came to the top of a steep hill on the route home. My daughter stopped her bike at the edge of the hill. She looked down the steep grade and got off the bike. "I think I will walk my bike down the hill," she said cautiously.

"Maureen," I said, "I know that you have the ability to ride your bike down that hill."

Maureen looked at me as if I was crazy. That hill looked like a cliff to her. "Dad," she said, "I can't do it."

"I tell you what," I said. "Why don't you ride your bike a few feet down the hill and then get off and walk it the rest of the way? You can use your brakes to go real slow."

Maureen paused. She wasn't so sure. "I don't think I can do that, Dad."

"I will walk beside you to make sure you don't fall off," I offered.

Maureen looked at me intently. In that moment, I knew that my daughter was weighing her trust of her father against the steepness of that hill. Hesitantly, Maureen agreed and gingerly got back on the bicycle. With my arms on her shoulders the whole time, she slowly rode down the hill about fifteen feet and then stopped. Maureen got off and she and I walked the rest of the way down the hill.

On our walk the next night, we had the same dilemma at the top of the hill. But this time with me at her side, Maureen rode about twenty-five feet down the hill, and then got off. The next night, she rode forty feet. And the next night, sixty feet.

By the end of the week, Maureen was riding her bike all the way down the hill.

Maureen did not believe that she could ride her bike down that hill. But I knew that she could do it with some encouragement and some assistance. If I had not been there to help her, Maureen might still be walking her bicycle down that steep hill.

A good teacher encourages the impossible. He prepares the disciple to do things that are unthinkable for that disciple. As I look back on my life and ministry, I know that I am doing things now that fifteen years ago I would have considered impossible. I am glad, though, that God allowed me to learn in stages - a step at a time.

Good teaching builds step by step. The teacher meets the disciple at his level, and assists him in getting to the next level. In a progression, the teacher lays a foundation and then slowly adds layer after layer of growth. A good teacher insures a solid foundation of doctrine; encourages personal growth in Christian disciplines and lifestyle; and helps the disciple discern his role - where that disciple belongs in the work of the Kingdom.

Good teaching is a gradual process. It requires patience and discernment by the teacher. The teacher must help discern what gifts and abilities the disciple possesses. Then the teacher must consider the steps the disciple needs to take to reach maturity in ministry. Step by step - stage by stage - the disciple grows as he prepares for a vibrant ministry. Learning by example, instruction and participation, the disciple achieves new levels of ministry and boldness.

PRINCIPLE: Teaching encourages growth step by step.

Good teaching leads to maturity. "And we proclaim Him, admonishing every man and *teaching every man with all wisdom*, that we may present every man complete in Christ." Col. 1:28.

APPLICATION

As a coach, I see myself as a teacher. It is my job to prepare young men to play soccer as a team. As such, I decided to become an instructor to my players.

At the first practice, the young men showed up with their gear - shirts, shorts, shin guards and cleats. I had something else in mind. We didn't practice on a field. I took my young men to a classroom and sat them down to listen and to learn.

Over the next few weeks in the classroom, I explained to my young men how the game of soccer was played. I shared with them about the skills they needed - the ways to dribble, pass and shoot. We talked about moves with the ball and team movement without

the ball.

I also illustrated the game to them. Lecturing with a blackboard, we went over formations - where I expected each player to be and how to handle game situations - throw ins, corner kicks, goal kicks, free kicks and penalty kicks. Videotape is illustrative, so we watched professional soccer teams perform. Images of great teams in action filled my players' heads.

Next, I exhorted the team. I wanted to inspire them to effective action. Hustle and enthusiasm are important, so my words focused on effort and exertion. I urged my players to give "110%" at all times.

Finally, attitude is important. I told my team that they could be great. They could do the very things that they had seen and heard through my classroom teaching. The players had the ability to perform just like the professional teams that they watched. I wanted my team to be confident and perhaps most importantly, to feel good about themselves.

By the time the first game came, I told them they were ready. Confident in our preparations, I gave my team the game time and directions to the playing field. I myself went home and did not go to the game, but I told my players that we would meet again next week in the classroom to discuss how they did, and to "teach" some more.

Did I do a good job of preparation? Was I a good teacher? Did my players now learn how to play soccer? How do you think they fared in the first game? Do you think they even showed up?

"Teaching" is a difficult concept. A part of teaching imparts knowledge. In teaching, words and images are important. That is instruction. Instruction is what I did in the classroom with my soccer team. But what good is knowledge if we don't know how to put it into practice?

Training is also a part of teaching. Training applies knowledge through practice and participation. Would not my soccer team have learned much more if they had the opportunity to put my instruction into practice under my watchful eye? Likewise, training in ministry is a necessary component of discipleship just as training in soccer is necessary to learn how to play it. Training translates knowledge into action so that a person learns by experience in addition to instruction.

PRINCIPLE: Effective teaching imparts knowledge and application.

There is a catch: It is more difficult to train than to preach. We can preach in large numbers. In fact, we tend to measure the success of the preaching by the numbers that come to hear us. Effective training, however, requires small numbers.

My concern is that our ministries focus heavily on the "classroom" - spoken and visual instruction about kingdom life. From the pulpit, we hear wonderful wisdom about Christian life, doctrine and ministry. Then we are exhorted to go out, apply the lesson on our own, and report back next Sunday for further instruction.

My encouragement is to emphasize training as much as instruction - to incorporate participation and application into teaching ministry. Only through effective training can a disciple complete the cycle of discipleship.

PRINCIPLE: Effective ministry preparation requires the sacrifice of ego.

MEDITATION: "For though by this time you ought to be teachers, you have need again for someone to teach you the elementary principles of the oracles of God, and you have come to need milk and not solid food." Heb. 5:12.

1. Do you sense the frustration of the writer of Hebrews?

2. Do you agree with the implication in this verse that mature Christians should be teachers?

3. What does good teaching mean to you?

4. Have you ever known a good teacher of ministry?

5. How did that teacher prepare disciples for ministry?

6. In what ways were you able to apply the teaching from that person?

REVIEW:

1. God calls us to make disciples who make disciples.
2. Call dwells in the heart of the disciple.
3. Preparing a disciple for ministry requires individual attention.
4. Teaching encourages growth step by step.
5. Effective teaching imparts knowledge and application.
6. Effective ministry preparation of others requires the sacrifice of ego.

SECTION THREE

THE CYCLE OF DISCIPLESHIP

LESSON 10 - THE GOAL

In soccer, a goal is huge. In professional soccer, goals are rare. At the highest levels, it is not unusual for both teams to play a 90 minute game and the result to be 0-0 ("nil nil").

The importance of a soccer goal is illustrated by the joy of the players who score them. One player takes a running start and does a "hands free" back flip after a goal. Another player sprints to the corner flag after a goal and starts kicking it as if he is shooting multiple times, then caps his celebration with a head butt of the flag.

After scoring a goal, the Spaniard, Fernando Torres, runs toward the stands with his thumb up to his mouth, demonstrating his nickname, El Nino - "the kid."

Dmitar Berbatov motions for his teammates to join him as he dashes toward the sideline. Side by side, they dive headfirst on their stomachs and slide along the grass toward the stands. Then they lift both hands as if to say "Ta Da!"

Broadcasters appreciate the importance of a goal. British announcers temporarily suspend their typical English reserve when a goal is scored: "He shoots. It's in the net! Brilliant! It's a brilliant goal! What a cracking boot by Stevie Gerard from thirty yards! An aMAZing shot! Absolutely priceless! The English national has done it again! Surely this must be the dagger in the heart of his opponents!"

Sportscasters south of the border are even less restrained. One announcer has a trademark"Goooooooooooooooooooooooooooooooooooooooooooooooooooooooooooooooooooo ooooooooooooooooooooooooooooooooooooooooooooooooooooooooooooooooooooooooal!" His extended rendition of the word lasts for thirty seconds or longer. He often takes breaths in the middle of the "o" to make the word last as long as the players' celebration.

Another announcer just repeats the word. "Goal! Goal! Goal! Goal! Goal! Goal! Goal! Goal! Goal! Goal! Goal! Goal! Goal! Goal! Goal! Goal! Goal! GOAL!"

The fans know how important a goal is. They stand during most of the game - chanting, singing, cheering, stomping and clapping. When a goal is scored, the team's fans break into elated pandemonium - roaring, screaming, dancing and clapping. It is a moment of delirious glee.

The most revered goal is the "golden goal." Most league soccer games can end in a tie. Even games in the group stage of a tournament can draw. However, a tournament elimination game - and particularly a championship game - require a winner. If the game is tied in regulation, the teams play overtime. The next goal is a "golden goal." It is climactic. The goal ends the game and determines the winner.

A golden goal is a moment of bedlam. Fans in the stands scream, hug, and shed tears of joy. Teammates on the field, and players and coaches from the bench, sprint toward the ecstatic goal scorer. They rush him so forcefully that their collective momentum knocks the whole group to the ground. What you see is a mound of humans piled on top of one another. It is a wonder that more players are not injured in the celebration.

In soccer, a goal is huge.

Our ministry has a goal. That goal far surpasses a goal in soccer. Our goal is eternal and incorruptible. It transcends time and space.

First, our goal is individual. Our goal is that every person grows into maturity in Christ. God desires that every man becomes complete in Christ. "And we proclaim Him, admonishing every man and teaching every man with all wisdom, that we may present every man **complete in Christ**." Col. 1:28.

Part of that completeness is that every person fulfills the call that God has for his life. God has a destiny - a ministry and calling for each follower. Our goal is for that destiny to be fulfilled. "For we are His workmanship, created in Christ Jesus for good works, which God prepared beforehand, that we should walk in them." Eph. 2:10.

Second, our goal is corporate. God has a plan for His church. At one point when He appears, He will "present to Himself the church in all her glory, having no spot or wrinkle or any such thing; but that she should be holy and blameless." Eph. 5:27. It is preparation of a pure, righteous and holy Bride. "This mystery is great." Eph. 5:32.

God has a destiny for His church - His body. That destiny is the fullness of Christ - the full embodiment of Christ in every aspect and dimension that reflects Who Christ is in all His glory and Being. "And He put all things in subjection under His feet, and gave Him as head over all things to the church, which is His body, **the fullness of Him who fills all in all.**" Eph. 1:22-23.

How do we get there? We function in the tools that God has given us in order to reach these goals. By His grace, God has given gifts for the church to use with purpose.

"And He gave some as apostles, and some as prophets, and some as evangelists, and some as pastors and teachers, for the equipping of the saints for the work of service, to the building up of the body of Christ; until we all attain to the unity of the faith, and of the knowledge of the Son of God, to a mature man, to the measure of the stature which belongs to the fullness of Christ." Eph. 4:11-13.

EQUIPPED

Boyz Club was formed to help foreign refugee youth living in an American inner city environment. The Club included Bosnian, Somalian, Vietnamese, Congolese and Liberian young men. Many of the young men had been in America only a few months. They were unfamiliar with American language, culture or custom. The Club served as an outlet for the young men, and helped them adjust to their life in the inner city.

The Boyz Club leaders planned field trips for members as a reward for regular attendance and good behavior. One of the earliest Boyz Club field trips visited a Halloween "haunted tour." The venue of the tour was a suburban park. Over the course of the walking tour, exhibitions and dramas were strategically placed along the path to frighten and entertain the young people on the tour.

At one location suitable for an ambush, a costumed "gorilla" jumped out of the woods and roared. Normally, children screamed and took off running down the path as the gorilla chased them. The Boyz Club group, however, was not a normal group.

As the Boyz Club group approached, the "gorilla" sprung out of the woods - growling and beating its chest. The boys stopped, but they didn't run. The "gorilla" paused for a moment - perplexed. He obviously was not accustomed to this sort of reaction. The

boys looked at each other, and then as one, started yelling and running toward the gorilla. The "gorilla" turned and ran back into the woods as the boys chased him.

By the time the Boyz Club leaders caught up with the group, the boys had tackled the "gorilla" and wrestled him to the ground. They were beating the poor guy. The leaders pulled the boys off of the stunned "gorilla," and with a few profound apologies, hustled the group back to the tour as quickly as they could.

Later, I spoke with Hunter, one of the Boyz Club leaders. "Hunter," I asked, "what brought that on?"

"I don't know," Hunter replied, shaking his head. "I am not sure what a gorilla means in Africa or Asia. I think that the boys were just being who they are."

"Just being who they are." God has a role for each of us. He has given us each wonderful gifts with which to serve Him and His purposes. We need to be who we are in Him. "And He gave some as apostles, and some as prophets, and some as evangelists, and some as pastors and teachers, for the **equipping** of the saints for the work of service, to the building up of the body of Christ;" Eph. 4:11-12.

God has equipped His saints to fulfill their destiny in Him. Ephesians 4 lists five different functions (apostle, prophet, evangelist, pastor, and teacher) given to the Body. These functions equip the saints for ministry. Each of these five functions is necessary for the Body of Christ to fulfill its destiny in Him.

PRINCIPLE: The five functions are given to equip the saints for effective ministry.

I. SENT BY GOD (Apostolic) - The word "apostle" literally means "a person sent from" or "a person sent away." An apostle can be a messenger or an envoy. Epaphroditus is called an "apostle" in Philippians 2:25. When God sends any person, that person is an envoy sent by God for His purpose. That person functions apostolically.

Sometimes in the New Testament, "apostle" is a special designation for Jesus' twelve disciples. Rev. 21:14. This authority should be honored and not demeaned or diminished. After all, Jesus personally called, trained and sent those twelve men into the world as apostles.

But the role or function of apostleship in the body of Christ is not limited to the Twelve. Otherwise, Paul would not be an apostle as well. "For I consider myself not in the least inferior to the most eminent apostles." II Cor. 11:5. I won't belabor the definition of an "apostle" here. Like many words in the Bible, the word "apostle" in scripture has different meanings in different contexts.

A person, however, whom God sends with a call to accomplish God's purpose *functions* like an apostle. Many persons are sent to establish a work of ministry. That apostolic function exists today. God is still a sending God.

II. WITH DIRECTION (Prophetic) - A prophet literally means "a person who speaks before" - a "foreteller." A prophet is a proclaimer and interpreter of divine revelation. The revelation is not limited to a future event. A prophetic function gives direction to a person or to a group - especially future direction. Any disciple who gives direction from God functions like a prophet.

III. TO MAKE CONTACT FOR SHARING (Evangelical) - In the context of Christ, sharing always implies the gospel. "For even though we, or angel from heaven, should preach to you a gospel contrary to that which we have preached to you, let him be accursed." Gal. 1:8. An evangelist is a "good newser." He preaches the gospel unto salvation.

A person who evangelizes often has "people-gifts." He has the ability to connect - to make contact - in order to proclaim. Permanence may be encouraged more by other gifts, but the evangelical function is necessary nonetheless. Any disciple who shares the gospel in word or in deed functions like an evangelist.

IV. FOR CARING (Pastoral) –

Here is a challenge: Find the word "pastor" in the Bible. Take your time.

The answer: In most English translations, the word "pastor" does not exist. The word "pastors" appears in most translations just one time - in Ephesians 4:11, the scripture

quoted above.

In fact, the word translated "pastors" in Ephesians 4:11 is really another word. It is the Greek word for "shepherds." Ephesians 4:11 literally says "And He gave some as apostles, and some as prophets, and some as evangelists, and some as shepherds and teachers..." The same word "shepherd" appears many times in the Bible.

A shepherd cares for a flock of sheep. Paul tells the elders at Ephesus "shepherd the church of God." Acts 20:28. Peter gives a similar instruction to elders. "Furthermore, I exhort the elders among you, as your fellow-elder...shepherd the flock of God..." I Pet. 5:1-2.

A shepherd in the kingdom of God is a person who cares for the lives of other persons. A shepherd undertakes responsibility for the spiritual and physical welfare of those persons. That responsibility alone is reason to give every pastoral office the respect due to it. That being understood, any disciple who shows responsible nurture and care for another disciple *functions* like a shepherd.

V. AND FOR PREPARING (Teaching) - God has called us to prepare disciples for kingdom life and ministry. A teacher prepares disciples for life and ministry. The rabbinic tradition is instructive here. Under the rabbinic tradition, a rabbi had a group of followers - disciples, if you will. The followers spent years with the rabbi. They went through stages of instruction and training. They learned by watching the rabbi and spending many hours in work and discourse with him.

Think of Jesus and His disciples. Jesus was the true Rabbi. "And the two disciples heard him speak, and they followed Jesus. And Jesus turned, and beheld them following, and said to them, 'What do you seek?' and they said to Him, 'Rabbi (which translated means Teacher), where are you staying?' He said to them, "Come and you will see.'" Jn. 1:37-39a. Any disciple who helps another disciple grow in faith or in ministry functions like a teacher.

The five functions in Ephesians 4:11 are tools that God has given us to fulfill the work to which He has called us. Through call, we understand to what work we are called, and how we should function in our gifts on a daily basis to fulfill that call.

Paul knew the callings with which he had been called. "And for this I was appointed a preacher and an apostle (I am telling the truth, I am not lying) as a teacher of the Gentiles in faith and truth." I Tim. 2:7. Paul was appointed an apostle, an evangelist, and a teacher of the Gentiles. As we read through the Book of Acts, we see Paul in action in these different roles as the situation required.

PRINCIPLE: The five functions are tools through which we fulfill our call.

"TO EACH ONE OF US, GRACE WAS GIVEN"

We tend to think of the tools that God has given - apostle, prophet, evangelist, pastor or teacher - in terms of an office or a position, in part because these offices have existed historically. Within the context of Ephesians 4, though, the five roles - apostle, prophet, evangelist, shepherd and teacher - are described as "gifts." "But to each one of us grace was given according to the measure of *Christ's gift*...And He *gave* some as apostles..." Eph. 4:7; 11a.

A gift from God is precious. It is given by grace. It should not be taken lightly. God's gift belongs to Him, not to us. We do not possess it.

A gift from God has a purpose. God's gift should be exercised conscientiously. "Handle with care." The gift should be used for the purpose intended. Remember that the gift is not the goal. The goal is completeness individually, and fullness corporately. The gift is only the means to the goal. At some point, the gifts will cease. I Cor. 13:8. A follower of Christ focuses on the task appointed by the Master. The follower is only an obedient servant.

The gifts are given by grace according to measure. The gifts are given in the exact measure needed to fulfill God's call. The grace given in the form of Christ's gift will be sufficient to meet the need of the moment.

PRINCIPLE: The five functions are gifts, not prestige.

"WALK WORTHY OF THE CALLING..."

Here is a dream described by a close friend:

I had a vision in the night. After being awakened and pondering it, I went back to sleep and was reawakened by the voice of the Shepherd, who spoke directly to me about it.

In the initial vision, I watched candidates for positions come forth. The Rabbi stood beside me and spoke to me about their authority. The candidates wanted positions of authority.

Then the voice of the Lord added the word "responsibility." That formed the crux of my vision. The mere position did not confer the authority needed. The position conferred responsibility. After that, acquiring the authority depended on how the man discharged his responsibility. The better the handling of the responsibility, the more extensive the authority acquired.

I believe the Keeper of the Vineyard suffers a "disappointment" that men arrogate to themselves fictional, or effete, authority. The cause of their fictional, or effete, authority is that they have failed to take seriously many tasks that their position required.

"I, therefore, the prisoner of the Lord, entreat you to walk in a manner worthy of the calling with which you have been called, with all humility and gentleness, with patience, showing forbearance to one another in love, being diligent to preserve the unity of the Spirit in the bond of peace." Eph. 4:1-3.

God has called each of us. Paul urges us to have the proper attitude with regard to our call. "Walk in a manner worthy of the calling with which you have been called."

Our society focuses on position, status and prestige. Man craves power. An office or position makes us powerful. "I am the pastor" or "I am an apostle." It is a position that we own, and we jealously guard the prestige that goes with it. This attitude is not consistent with "all humility and gentleness, with patience, showing forbearance to one another in love..."

Jesus' two disciples, James and John, wanted positions of prestige, power, and glory.

"Grant that we may sit in Your glory, one on Your right and one on Your left." Mk. 10:37.

Jesus' response was telling. "You do not know what you are asking for. Are you able to drink the cup that I drink, or to be baptized with the baptism with which I am baptized?" Mk. 10:38.

Jesus is saying "You clearly do not understand. Position brings responsibility. The positions you request have dire consequences. Let's talk about the responsibility before we talk about the positions themselves." Ironically, after Jesus established that James and John would bear the required responsibility - "My cup you shall drink..." (Mt. 20:23a), He still did not grant them the requested positions.

I had never met Tim, but I had heard much about his ministry to the homeless. He was the scheduled speaker at a church meeting, so I went a little early in order to talk with him.

"Good to meet you," Tim said. "What is your position here?"

I paused self-consciously. "Um...I really don't have a position here."

"Oh!" Tim said. "What is your title?"

"Well..." I hesitated again. "I don't have a title here either. The guys call me 'Coach' so I guess you can say that is my title."

Tim seemed a little perplexed. "Well..." He seemed at a loss for words. "Well...what do you do?"

My eyes brightened. Here was a question that I could answer! "What do I do? Let me tell you...." And I proceeded to give Tim a full description of our ministry and what we did.

Function trumps status. Responsibility triumphs over title. God is no respecter of persons. Acts 10:34 (ASV). Instead He "impartially judges according to each man's *work*." I Pet. 1:17.

PRINCIPLE: Responsibility and function define position in the Kingdom.

GIFTS AND AUTHORITY

God has all authority, so God is the source of all authority. A gift from God is not just a function given by Him. It is a type of authority being shared by Him. "And God has appointed in the church, first apostles, second prophets, third teachers, then miracles..." I Cor. 12:28. God appoints. A spiritual gift is not cause for personal glory. It is a grant of authority given by God.

PRINCIPLE: A gift is an area of authority established by God.

The proper response to any authority is an attitude of submission. Rom. 13:1. We respect the authority, not because of the person who possesses it, but because we recognize the authority as from God. Thus, any spiritual gift should be respected as authority given by God.

RESOURCE

For years, a small group of us worked in the neighborhood. The harder we worked, the more the needs seemed to grow. At times, we felt overwhelmed. There was no way that we could fulfill the ministry laid before us.

We began concerted and intentional prayer for help. We asked the Lord to send workers into the harvest. Gradually, the Lord sent ministers with a common vision to the same work. It encouraged us for the workers to arrive, and it built our faith to see our prayers answered.

What we eventually realized is that God did not just bring new people to the work. God gave us new gifts to enhance the work. Each person brought talents and abilities to the table, along with faith. Our work not only grew, but our work became more mature - more complete.

When we respect a gift, then we are in a position to receive its benefit. A gift of God is not given primarily for the benefit of its recipient. A gift of God is given for the benefit of His church. "But to each one is given the manifestation of the Spirit for the common good." I Cor. 12:7. The gift is a resource for the benefit of the Body.

PRINCIPLE: The five roles are gifts to the Body of Christ.

We know that this fact is particularly true for the five gifts of Ephesians 4. Paul not only describes the gifts, but Paul tells us the wonderful benefits to the Body from the proper function of those gifts - benefits like equipping, growth, unity, knowledge, maturity, and finally fullness.

PRINCIPLE: Each fivefold gift is a resource for the Body.

How do we receive maximum benefit from a gift? This part is sometimes hard to swallow. Just as we receive benefit from authority by submitting to it -"It is a minister of God to you for good." Rom. 13:4, we receive benefit from a gift of God by submitting to the gift. As Paul encouraged the Ephesians, "Be subject to one another in the fear of Christ." Eph. 5:21. When we submit to a gift as an area of authority from God, we receive benefit from the authority of that gift.

Submission is a key to successful ministry preparation. If you feel called to minister in a certain area, one beneficial thing that you can do is locate another person experienced and functioning in that area of ministry, and submit yourself to him. Spend time with that person - a lot of time - watching, listening, learning - and doing.

PRINCIPLE: Benefit from a gift is received through submission to it.

MEDITATION: "For I am confident of this very thing, that He who began a good work in you will perfect it until the day of Christ Jesus." Phil. 1:6.

1. What does "complete in Christ" mean to you personally?

2. What would it look like if you were "complete in Christ?"

3. Do you see yourself in any of the five functions described in this chapter?

4. What steps can you take to grow in those functions?

REVIEW:

1. Our ministry has a goal.

2. Our goal is individual - that every person would grow into completeness in Christ.

3. Our goal is corporate. The destiny of the church is the fullness of Christ.

4. The five functions fully equip the saints to reach these goals.

5. The five functions are tools through which we fulfill our call.

6. The five functions are gifts, not prestige.

7. Responsibility and function define position in the Kingdom.

8. A gift is an area of authority established by God.

9. Each fivefold gift is a resource for the Body of Christ.

10. Benefit from a gift is received through submission to it.

THE CYCLE OF DISCIPLESHIP

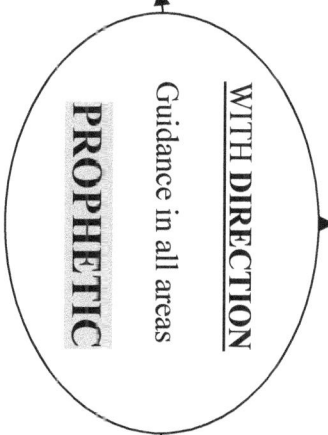

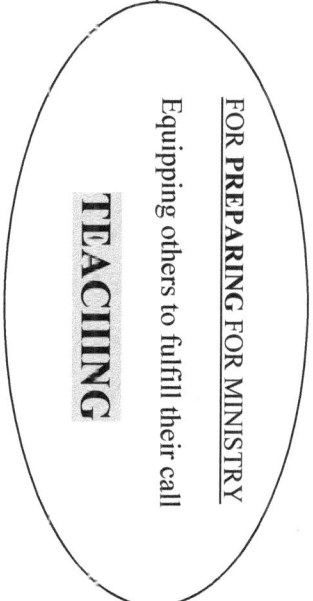

EVANGELICAL

FOR THE PURPOSE OF SHARING

The gospel of Jesus Christ

And develop relationship

TO MAKE CONTACT
With other people

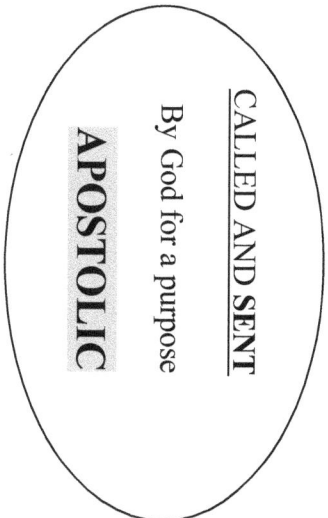

PASTORAL

FOR THE PURPOSE OF CARING

And helping others to heal and to grow

PROPHETIC

WITH **DIRECTION**

Guidance in all areas

APOSTOLIC

CALLED AND SENT

By God for a purpose

RELEASE INTO MINISTRY

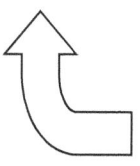

TEACHING

FOR **PREPARING FOR MINISTRY**

Equipping others to fulfill their call

125

LESSON 11- THE CYCLE OF DISCIPLESHIP

How do I judge the success of coaching for a season? "Wins and losses" is the obvious standard. But "wins and losses" is not my main goal. My overriding standard for team success on the field is whether each player has improved individually as a player and as a person (equipping), and whether the team has improved its play as a whole (corporate growth).

Some of my teams had excellent won/loss records. But, based on improvement and growth, I considered some of my least talented teams as some of the most successful ones.

My son played on a team from a different school one year that struggled. His old coach departed the prior year, and with him went some of the team's best players. The next season, my son's team had a record of 1 win and 13 losses. Afterwards, he and I discussed the season.

"Son," I said, "I think your coach did a great job. That was a very successful season."

My son looked at me like I was crazy. "What do you mean?" he asked.

"Look at your last three games."

"We lost our last three games."

"Yes," I replied. "But look at who you played. First, you played a team that beat you 5-0 earlier in the season. But the score of the second game with that team was 3-1. Next, you played a team that beat you 6-0 in the first game. The score of the second game was 2-1."

My son listened intently.

"Finally, in the playoffs, you played a team that had beaten you 9-0 and 7-1 in the regular season. But the playoff game was a hard fought, evenly matched tilt. You lost that game 1-0 by a goal scored in the last five minutes - and that goal was an own goal.

"By the last game, your team was a different team. It had improved immensely by the last game."

"And he gave some as apostles, and some as prophets, and some as evangelists, and some as pastors and teachers, for the equipping of the saints for the work of service, to the **building up** of the body of Christ; until we all attain to the unity of the faith, and of the knowledge of the Son of God, to a mature man, to the measure of the stature which belongs to the fullness of Christ." Eph. 4:11-13.

As we walk on our journey with the Lord through the years, we realize His deep mercy and love in the manner that He deals with us. He accepts us and loves us where we are. We may have 1 win and 13 losses for a season, but God lavishes grace upon us to improve. He allows us to work with our present gifts, and He helps us to grow in those gifts. Along the way, God may give us more gifts. It is a gradual progression of growth.

The growth of the church is also a progression. The five functions - apostles, prophets, evangelists, pastors and teachers - are the gifts that God gives to help the church to grow and reach maturity. These gifts function in a sequence causing body growth.

God sends a disciple (apostolic function) to make contact with other people. That disciple (or other disciples working with him) shares the gospel with other people (evangelical) leading to conversion. The new believer(s) then receive healing and care (shepherding) and as growth occurs, undergo preparation for ministry (teaching). Then the Lord calls (prophetic) the believer(s) who have now grown and been equipped for ministry. The Lord sends them (apostolic function) to make contact with other people, and the cycle begins anew. Each step of the process is guided by the Lord (prophetic).

It is a cycle that grows the body numerically by adding new believers to the church. It is a cycle that also grows body members to maturity as each believer grows in gift(s) given to him.

> PRINCIPLE: The fivefold gifts work together in a progression.

THE FOUNDATION OF THE APOSTOLIC

I was seeking guidance from a man that I loved and admired. "Pastor Late," I asked, "what is authority?"

As he often did, Pastor Late paused before answering. He then said "'Authority' comes from the word root 'author.' The author of something - its founder - has authority over it. An inventor controls his invention because it came from him. He has authority over it because he can make it work. God has authority over the universe, and everything in it, because he created it."

Pastor Late had experience in the area of authority. He did not found the church that he pastored, but he did lead it into a new dimension. In the early 1970's, the Lord poured His Spirit upon that congregation - and the body grew in numbers and in maturity. Pastor Late led the church during this growth.

A few years after he retired, the church recognized Pastor Late's role in a new way. The church asked Pastor Late to function in an apostolic role in advising and serving the leadership of the church.

"So then you are no longer strangers and aliens, but you are fellow-citizens with the saints, and are of God's household, having been built upon **the foundation of the apostles and prophets**, Christ Jesus Himself being the corner stone, in Whom the whole building, being fitted together is growing into a holy temple in the Lord..." Eph. 2:19-21.

All ministries need a foundation. The church is built upon a foundation of apostles and prophets. Analogously today, the function of apostle and prophet are foundational to the work of the church. The apostle has been sent by God to perform a work. He often is the founder of a work. As founder of that work, the apostle possesses authority in that area of work.

Paul was adamant about his authority as an apostle to the churches he founded. Paul "aspired to preach the gospel, not where Christ was already named, that I might not build upon another man's foundation." Rom. 15:20. Paul knew that where he founded and built, he possessed apostolic authority. He reminded the Corinthian church "If to others I am not an apostle, at least I am to you; for you are the seal of my apostleship in the Lord." I Cor. 9:2.

THE FOUNDATION OF THE PROPHETIC

When you coach diverse nationalities on a soccer team, communication is one of the biggest challenges. I once coached a team that had players from nine different nations (Yemen, Somalia, Bosnia, Serbia, Congo, Liberia, Mexico, USA, and Vietnam). Sometimes we struggled to communicate, but we had a lot of fun. That season was an enriching and culturally broadening experience for those young men. Many of them are still close friends.

Our communication issues could be an advantage or a disadvantage. One year, my team was playing in an extremely close match against one of our rivals. Both defenses played well and at halftime, it was a scoreless tie.

In the middle of the second half, the opposing team sent a cross into our penalty area right in front of our own goal. Both my American goalkeeper and a Vietnamese defender had the ability to get to the ball and clear it out of danger. They miscommunicated, though, and neither went for the ball. An opponent swooped in between them and tapped the ball into the goal. We were losing 1-0.

Both teams fought hard as we tried to equalize. Near the end of the game, the other team committed a foul about thirty yards from the goal and the referee awarded us a free kick. Elvir was Bosnian and I told him to take the kick. He had to decide whether to pass the ball into the penalty area or to shoot it. It was a long shot, but I knew that Elvir had the ability to make it. I decided our communication issues could be used to an advantage. I turned to Fahret, another Bosnian on our bench, and softly said, "Fahret, tell Elvir to shoot the ball in your language."

Fahret yelled at Elvir something that sounded like "Shutai."

Elvir understood and took the shot. It was a beautiful, curving ball that soared past the goalkeeper into the upper right corner of the goal. That goal salvaged a tie in an important match.

A few years later, we faced a similar situation. Our team was awarded a long, free kick. Mohamed was going to take the kick, and I knew he could make it from there. I felt the same ploy was in order and turned to Isak on the bench.

"Isak," I said secretively with my back turned toward the other team's bench.

"Yes, Coach."

"Tell Mohamed to shoot the ball." I spoke softly so the other team could not hear me.

"You want me to tell Mohamed to shoot the ball?"

"Yes" I whispered furtively. "Tell Mohamed 'Shoot the ball.'"

"Okay, Coach" Isak said. He walked to the sideline, put his hands to his mouth and loudly yelled "Hey! Mohamed! SHOOT THE BALL!"

I buried my head in my hands. Isak did exactly what I had told him.

Communication is vital to any enterprise. In our case, the enterprise is the kingdom of God. Communication from the King is vital. This role belongs to the prophetic gift. The prophetic is foundational because it provides guidance and direction for the other four functions.

Without the prophetic, the other four functions have no direction. The prophetic is the difference between Jonah going to Nineveh, Jonah going to Tarshish, or Jonah just wandering aimlessly and ineffectually anywhere. The modern day Jonah may be going the wrong way because of disobedience or out of simple ignorance. Without the prophetic, however, that Jonah does not know that God wants him to go to Nineveh. The prophetic feeds all other functions.

PRINCIPLE: The apostolic and prophetic are foundational to the other three gifts.

On the next page is a chart that illustrates the foundational nature of the apostolic and the prophetic in relation to the functional progression of the fivefold gifts. Take time to review it.

THE CYCLE OF DISCIPLESHIP

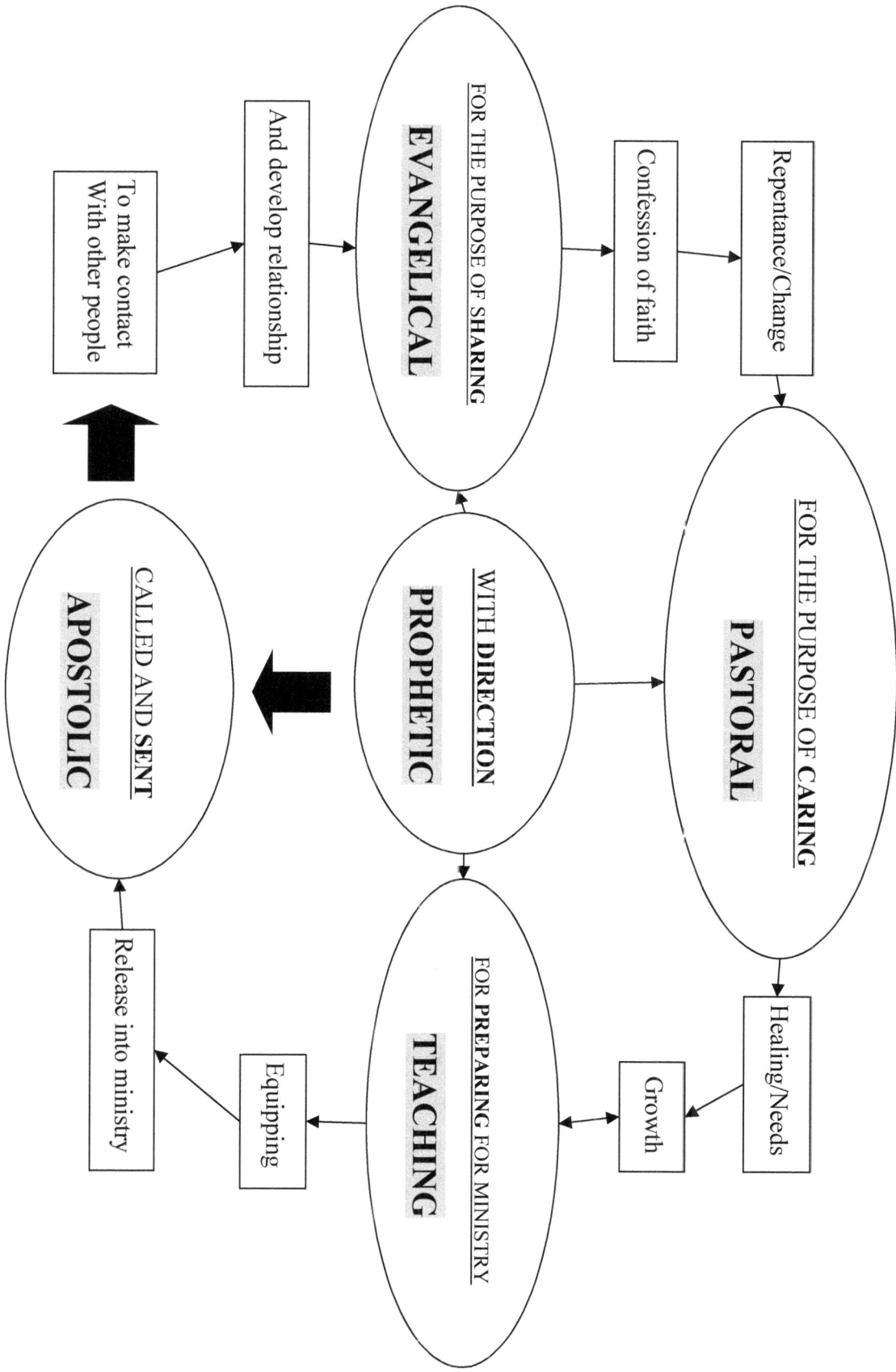

EVANGELICAL

FOR THE PURPOSE OF SHARING

To make contact
With other people

And develop relationship

Confession of faith

Repentance/Change

PASTORAL

FOR THE PURPOSE OF CARING

PROPHETIC

WITH DIRECTION

APOSTOLIC

CALLED AND SENT

Release into ministry

TEACHING

FOR PREPARING FOR MINISTRY

Equipping

Growth

Healing/Needs

131

THE CYCLE OF DISCIPLESHIP

Note that effective completion of the cycle of discipleship requires all five functions.

A. God sends (apostolic) a disciple with direction (prophetic). He may be sent to a people group, a neighborhood, a city, a region, or even just to an individual. But that disciple makes contact with the person(s) to whom he is sent.

Often, contact is difficult because of cultural, linguistic, ethnic or religious barriers. But contact is necessary because it is a means to relationship. In this book, you have read numerous stories about soccer, which is a wonderful means of contact and relationship building for many reasons. But the pathways to contact are as numerous as the record of human activity. Any sport, hobby, occupation, recreation, endeavor or mutual point of connection is a means of contact.

As connections multiply, the relationship grows. The process is often slow, but when trust is built and the kingdom of God modeled, a platform is established. Relationship affords an opportunity. Relationship establishes a platform for sharing.

Relationship establishes a platform for sharing.

B. Through relationship, the disciple shares the gospel with the person(s) to whom the disciple is called (evangelical). The sharing occurs through word and through action. "Let your light shine before men in such a way that they may see your good works, and glorify your Father who is in heaven." Mt. 5:16. Through the Holy Spirit, sharing that is received leads to a confession of faith. "…with the heart man believes, resulting in righteousness, and with the mouth he confesses, resulting in salvation." Rom. 10:10.

This confession is a cause for rejoicing. But thereafter, the disciple looks for confirmation of faith through repentance. "I tell you that in the same way, there will more joy in heaven over one sinner who repents, than over ninety-nine righteous persons who need no repentance." Lk. 15:7. Repentance means change. The convert who believes performs "deeds appropriate to repentance." Acts 26:20. The disciple looks for change in lifestyle, change in personality, and change in the desires of the heart of the new believer. Is it real, or is it just religion of man?

> True repentance means change.

C. The disciple (or other disciples who have the needed gifts) ministers to the person who confesses and who changes his life through repentance. The disciple provides care (pastoral) and encourages growth (pastoral and teaching) for the new believer.

A major component of care is meeting personal needs and ministering healing. Many converts have been subjected to the ravages of sin. Before they can grow, they need help.

When I was in college, I sprained my ankle severely. The x-rays showed that no bones were broken, but my ankle looked as if a softball had grown on the outside of my foot. The pain was excruciating, and the words of comfort from my doctor were "It would be better if you had broken it."

But the doctor did not allow me to walk on the ankle initially. He put a tightly wrapped "pressure cast" on my ankle (also excruciating), and instructed me not to put any weight on the foot, but to use crutches. For two weeks, I used one good leg and my crutches to go anywhere. The doctor knew that the ligaments and muscles in my ankle needed to heal before I could begin to walk again.

After two weeks, the doctor removed the pressure cast, and put a "walking cast" on my leg. The walking cast was a plaster boot around my foot and up my shin that had a rubber stob encased below my heel. I painfully walked around like I had a "peg leg." Every night, my ankle had swelled inside of the boot so that it pressed hard against the sides of the cast. Every morning, after my foot had been elevated during the night, the swelling went down and my foot and ankle were loose inside of the boot. The doctor knew that the ankle needed support to strengthen to the point that I could walk without assistance again.

After four weeks, the doctor cut away the cast and told me I was strong enough to walk on the ankle again. The ankle was still sore and still swelled during the day, but the day that cast was removed was a glorious day.

133

Just as my ankle need to heal before my muscles and ligaments could strengthen and grow, many people that come to the Lord need healing before they can strengthen and grow in the Lord. Some of the forms of healing include:

1. Healing of wounds and hurts in the person – in the body, the spirit and the emotions.
2. Meeting personal needs – such as hunger, clothing, shelter, and hygiene.
3. Correcting ungodly beliefs and mistaken views of God.
4. Altering dysfunctional behaviors.
5. Breaking destructive generational (or cultural) patterns.
6. Deliverance from spiritual oppressions and bondages.

After the ministry of care and healing, then growth (pastoral and teaching) can occur. Areas of growth include (these lists are not comprehensive):

1. Knowledge of what a Christian believes. (Sound doctrine)
2. Christian character. (Christlike traits)
3. Christian lifestyle. (Consistent godly living.)
4. Christian disciplines (Prayer, Bible study, worship, giving, fasting, etc.)
5. Development of discerned spiritual gifts.
6. Christian Ministry.

Think of a fruit tree. An apple seedling does not produce apples in the first year that it is planted - nor in the second year or third year. It only grows. In fact, an orchard apple tree needs to grow between 5-8 years before it begins to produce fruit. It is not always the case for the disciple, but usually there is a season of growth before the Lord calls and releases the disciple into fruitful ministry. But the growth occurs to prepare the disciple for call. "'Behold, for three years I have come looking for fruit on this tree without finding any. Cut it down! Why does it even use up the ground?' And he answered and said to him. 'Let it alone, sir, for this year too, until I dig around it and put in fertilizer…'" Lk. 13:7-8.

D. Care and growth are both provided with a view toward call. As the believer grows in the Lord, he learns how to discern the Lord's will for his life (prophetic). Cognizant of the believer's gifts and of the direction to which the believer feels called, the believer receives training for ministry (teaching). At the point that the believer is ready, a release occurs. God sends the believer (apostolic) into ministry with direction (prophetic)...and the cycle repeats itself. The believer becomes the person who makes disciples.

It is a cycle that should repeat over and over again. Remember that the call is to make disciples who make disciples.

Every body of believers or ministry needs this cyclical function. If the body fulfills this cycle, it is functional in the way that God intended. Conversely, if it does not fulfill this cycle, it is dysfunctional, and does not operate in the fullness that God intended.

The cycle needs to flow fully and completely. If one of the five functions is missing, the cycle is broken. It is impaired by a missing part. At times one function may be needed more than the others. At a specific moment, only one function may be needed. But all five functions applied at the proper time are necessary for the cycle to operate in a healthy and fruitful manner.

PRINCIPLE: Every body of believers needs all five gifts for the body to function properly.

IMBALANCE

I attended a congregational meeting at a church one time. What struck me was not the business of the church being conducted. What struck me was the composition of the membership in attendance.

That congregation was aging. I realized that most of the participants were elderly. In fact, as I surveyed further, I could only identify one person in that crowd that was under the age of forty. She was a young lady in her early twenty's. "Very strange!" I thought to myself.

As the meeting progressed, the lone young person rose to speak at the microphone - a very brave thing to do in that august group of older saints. The young lady made a plea. She said that the young people in the church needed help. The youth group was

floundering, and single adults lacked fellowship and training. Was the church willing to do more to assist and support the youth in the church?

As the young lady held the microphone, an older lady turned to her and emphatically said, "When we were young, we had to do things on our own! We formed our own groups and we had our own fellowship. You young people should do the same thing!"

Rebuffed and embarrassed, the young lady sat down meekly.

I left that meeting extremely grieved. Within a few weeks, the young lady left that church and sought fellowship elsewhere.

What happened in that meeting? A young believer made a plea. She was a growing Christian that desired teaching and training. The older lady, however, had a different focus. Her church emphasized care for its own members so heavily that concern for others was lacking. The well meaning pastoral staff, through its enveloping care, had enabled an attitude of selfishness to develop among the members of the congregation.

Please understand that care for members is a wonderful thing. Shepherding is a necessary fivefold function. In this case, however, the focus on shepherding was so strong that it overshadowed the function of teaching and training. The heavy emphasis on shepherding actually prevented the operation of the other gifts that God intended for the church. The gifts were out of balance.

"What?" a wise teacher once asked me. "What is heresy?"

"I don't know," I answered. "Maybe false doctrine?"

"My favorite definition of heresy," the teacher continued, "is this: Heresy is truth carried to an extreme."

That church struggled for many years. Its membership dwindled from 1500 to 400. The emphasis on shepherding truth was so extreme that it precluded the function of evangelical and training gifts needed to bring in young converts and to release mature disciples into ministry. The gifts were out of balance.

The cycle was broken.

MEDITATION: "[F]rom whom the whole body, being fitted and held together by that which every joint supplies, according to the proper working of each individual part, causes the growth of the body for the building up of itself in love." Eph. 4:16.

1. How does each of the five gifts contribute to the numerical growth of the body?

2. Have you ever experienced a functioning model of the sequence described in this chapter?

3. Why is proper balance of each gift necessary?

4. How can such separate and different gifts work together to cause growth?

REVIEW:

1. The fivefold gifts work together in a progression to grow the church numerically, and to mature followers of Christ.

2. The apostolic and prophetic are foundational to the other three gifts.

3. The apostolic, evangelical, shepherding, and teaching gifts work in sequence - all directed by the prophetic.

4. Relationship establishes a platform for sharing (evangelical).

5. A new believer needs care, healing and growth.

6. The cycle should repeat over and over again.

7. Every body of believers needs all five gifts for the Body to function properly.

8. If some of the gifts are missing or out of balance, the cycle is broken and growth is stunted.

LESSON 12 - EFFECTIVE FUNCTION

When was the first time that you realized that discipleship could be costly? The first time that you realized that strict obedience might demand crushing sacrifice?

We sponsored a large block party in the impoverished neighborhood near the church. This neighborhood was full of drugs, gangs and violent crime. With permission, we blocked off one of the streets and set up basketball goals. We put soccer goals in a side area, brought a large music system, and served food and drinks. During set up, I asked the organizer what else was needed. He asked me to go buy some ice for drinks for the participants.

I drove to the neighborhood convenience store on the corner. At the counter, I pulled out my wallet to pay for the ice. The front door opened. In walked a scruffy man wearing blue jeans and a T-shirt. His appearance is not what drew my attention, though. What drew my attention was the handle of the .38 caliber pistol that was protruding above the top of his jeans. As I stood there with my wallet in my hand, I perceived that the diminutive, foreign clerk behind the counter offered me no protection. For a moment, I had a stunning thought. I realized that day could be my last.

To my relief, the armed man walked to the cooler in the back of the store. He was just making a purchase, not a withdrawal. Keeping a wary eye on him, I hurriedly paid for the ice and exited the store.

Can God use tragedy of the worst type? Can He redeem even the murder of His saints?

The early church in Jerusalem overcame many challenges. They survived imprisonment (Acts 4:3), threats (Acts 4:21), and beatings (Acts 5:40) to build a vibrant, close knit community of believers (Acts 4:32ff). The church was thriving in Jerusalem.

Then Stephen was murdered because of his faith! Acts 7:60. Do you think that many believers in Jerusalem felt stunned as they realized that their faith could cost them their lives? Persecution arose, and their faith cost them their homes, their jobs and their security as they fled from Jerusalem. "And on that day a great persecution arose against the church in Jerusalem; and they were all scattered throughout the regions of Judea and Samaria, except the apostles." Acts

8:1b.

How could God possibly be working in this situation? Jesus had instructed His followers to "be My witnesses both in Jerusalem, and in all Judea and Samaria, and even to the remotest part of the earth." Acts 1:8. Until that time, His disciples had done a great job on that first leg, Jerusalem. Was God now prompting His church to fulfill the rest of His instructions?

A FIVEFOLD BODY

"So then those who were scattered because of the persecution that arose in connection with Stephen made their way to Phoenicia and Cyprus and Antioch, speaking the word to no one except to the Jews alone. But there were some of them, men of Cyprus and Cyrene, who came to Antioch and began speaking to the Greeks also, preaching the Lord Jesus." Acts 11:19-20.

One significant result of the death of Stephen was the founding of a church that operated in marvelous fivefold function. At Antioch, the cycle of discipleship through the five gifts blossomed. First, some saints that fled Jerusalem acted apostolically in that they went to Antioch. Granted, they probably were more "kicked out" of Jerusalem than sent. Sometimes, though, God has to nudge us in order to get us to go in His direction. Ask Jonah.

Next, those saints functioned evangelically. They made contact with the citizens of Antioch and preached the Lord Jesus. The preaching was effective. "And the hand of the Lord was with them, and a large number who believed turned to the Lord." Acts 11:21.

When the news of this mission reached the church at Jerusalem, they sent Barnabas (apostolic) to Antioch. Acts 11:22. Barnabas encouraged the church to "remain true to the Lord." Acts 11:23. Encouragement is a primary shepherding function. "And considerable numbers were brought to the Lord." (evangelism) Acts 11:24.

Barnabas saw this explosion as an opportunity for growth through teaching. He went to Tarsus and brought back Saul with him to Antioch. "And it came about that for an entire year they met with the church, and taught considerable numbers." Acts 11:26.

The work at Antioch received direction from the prophetic. Prophets came from Jerusalem to Antioch and one of them, Agabus, prophesied that a great famine would take place.

139

Acts 11:28. This prophetic word enabled the Antioch church to act providentially to alleviate the impact of this famine. Acts 11:29-30.

Through the cycle of fivefold function, the church at Antioch was founded and grew. To the greater glory of God, through the five gifts, the church at Antioch matured from a mission church to a "sending church." Acts 13:1 lists five leaders (Barnabas, Simeon, Lucius, Manaen, and Saul) that were "prophets and teachers." Through the mutual and cooperative ministry of these five men (fivefold function), the Lord called (prophetic) Barnabas and Saul to be sent (apostolic). "Set apart for Me Barnabas and Saul for the work to which I have called them." Acts 13:2. Thus began the "first missionary journey" on which many people in other areas were converted and churches in other places founded.

The importance of the church at Antioch in God's plan can not be overemphasized. Thenceforth, Paul used Antioch as his "base" and as the launching point for other missionary journeys. Paul and Barnabas returned to Antioch to report on the first missionary journey. "And they spent a long time with the disciples." Acts 14:26-28.

The second missionary journey launched from Antioch. "But Paul chose Silas and departed, being committed by the brethren to the grace of the Lord." Acts 15:35-40. Paul returned to Antioch from that second journey. Acts 18:22. "And having spent some time there [at Antioch], he departed..." Acts 18:23. Paul went forth again on the third journey.

The church at Antioch operated effectively in the five gifts. The saints used the five gifts cooperatively in a cycle of discipleship in Antioch itself. Then, through the prophetic and apostolic, the church sent Barnabas, Paul, Silas and others to make disciples "to the remotest part of the earth." The church at Antioch demonstrated Christlikeness.

"And the disciples were first called Christians in Antioch." Acts 11:26.

TAPPING GIFT RESOURCE

How does this type of cooperative ministry occur? How can we operate in effective fivefold function?

Barney was a close friend and coworker. Barney worked for a church. He had a

knack for getting things done. Ever pragmatic, Barney was a problem solver with the ability to transform limited resources into functioning operations.

Barney was the man responsible for the "miracle of the maple syrup." Barney helped us take fifteen Boyz Club members up to the mountains one February for a weekend retreat. To the wonderment of some boys that had never seen it before, snow fell the first night. The next day, we played snow football for four hours.

After football, we cooked pancakes and bacon for the guys. To our dismay, we discovered we only had half a bottle of maple syrup to feed eighteen hungry people. A trip to the store in the snow was out of the question. Barney, however, was on the job. He scrounged up a little Karo syrup, a little sugar and I don't know what else. Thanks to Barney, and Barney's gifts, we had plenty of maple syrup for everyone, and some left over besides.

Pragmatic people like Barney are rarely visionaries. I was having lunch one day with Barney when he expressed some stress from his job at the church. "I just don't feel that I can meet all the ministry needs at the church. We have so many things that need to be done, and that could be done. It is stressful at times."

"I understand," I said. "That is where guidance comes in. We need help from the Lord as far as specific direction."

"That is exactly what I mean," Barney replied. "How do you pick and choose? I feel stress because I can't decide which items to do."

"Barney, that is why we have different gifts in the body. You have wonderful gifts, but a prophetic function is not the strongest one. It may be an area into which you grow in the future, but it isn't there now. No wonder you feel stress. You were not intended to make those decisions alone. We feel stress when we try to function in an area in which we are not gifted. God calls us to function as a body. If you need direction and you don't have a prophetic gift, seek out persons in the body that have those gifts and avail yourself of their gift.

"The very people that you need," I continued, "also need you. Many prophetic people can't administrate or implement effectively. You need them for vision and direction, and they need you for implementation and action."

"And He gave some as apostles, and some as prophets, and some as evangelists, and some as pastors and teachers, for the equipping of the saints for the work of service, to the building up of the body of Christ; until we all attain to **the unity of the faith**, and of the knowledge of the Son of God, to a mature man, to the measure of the stature which belongs to the fullness of Christ." Eph. 4:11-13.

The fivefold gifts are cooperative. All five gifts are needed for the gifts to function properly. The gifts may be present in assorted groupings. There may be two, four, five, or eight people with the five gifts among them. Every person in the group, however, needs to submit to each respective gift to receive its benefit. Barney needed to submit to a prophetic gift in order to function properly, and vice versa. It is a reciprocal relationship. There may be multiple persons, but each person's gift is utilized in terms of resource.

> PRINCIPLE: Cooperative ministry yields resource.

Christians regularly struggle to submit to the gifts that God has given us. This struggle may occur for many dysfunctional reasons. Often, the reason we struggle to submit to the gift is the package that holds the gift. The gift itself may be precious and even needful, but we find the person that possesses the gift repulsive.

Alonso came from west Africa. He was an enthusiastic teenager with boundless energy. One of our most valuable ministry partners was the Charlotte Eagles Soccer Club. The Eagles loved to have groups of our soccer players attend their professional games. The Eagles' players were careful to encourage the young men.

Alonso came with us to one of the Eagles' games. After the boys got off the van, I noticed that Alonso disappeared for a little bit. When he returned the group, he had undergone a slight transformation. Alonso had brought a bottle of white liquid shoe polish and poured it over his head and face. The white shoe polish created quite an effect spread all over Alonso's dark hair and skin. Alonso looked "wild."

During the game, Alonso's actions matched his looks. He screamed and gyrated during the game. He led my group of guys in cheers and chants stomping on the metal stands for emphasis. Some other young men had brought barrels to the game to beat as drums. Alonso went over to the drummers and danced and pounded as the thumping pulsated across the field. Alonso then led the drummers back over to our group, and the noise volume increased considerably.

Thankfully, the Eagles won the game. After the game, the Eagles gathered in a "players only" huddle for prayer. Players only, that is, except for one white-faced African fan. Alonso ran into the huddle and was graciously included by the Eagles.

Based on Alonso's actions that evening, I wasn't sure that I wanted to claim him. Honestly, I was a little embarrassed.

A few days later, the president of the Charlotte Eagles called me. He discussed some other business. "By the way," he said, "thank you for bringing the guys out to the game. I was talking to some of the players. They felt more fan support during that game than any other game that they have played. They love it when you bring your guys."

When I hung up the phone, I had to reconsider my perceptions. Alonso's wildness didn't appeal to me. But he had clearly brought a great gift of encouragement to the players competing on the field. Strange packaging - but clearly an effective gift.

My wise grandmother once said "I looked and looked for the perfect church until I realized that, even if I found one, the minute I joined the church, it would become imperfect." Each of us should be grateful that God graciously shares His gifts with flawed persons such as us.

PRINCIPLE: By grace, God gives fantastic gifts to imperfect people.

Personality conflicts are inevitable. Many times, a particular personality manifests a specific gift. In a touch of irony and humbling need, the personality most repulsive to one gift often accompanies a different gift most needed by it. Barney, for example, is a "nuts and bolts" guy. He functions in "down to earth" application, and loves to teach and train others. Conversely, the prophetic personality that can assist Barney is often "up in the air," sometimes incomprehensible or even flighty. The thought processes are very different. The gifts and personalities may conflict, but the gifts require mutual cooperation.

PRINCIPLE: Grace is necessary both in the giving and the receiving of the gift.

Here are some gift traits - tempered by the truism that every person is different and the manifestation of each gift varies accordingly. In other words, please read the descriptions "with a grain of salt."

1. APOSTOLIC - An apostolic function is forward thinking, often visionary and operates outside of the box. Brave and daring, the apostolic personality does not shrink from new horizons. An apostolic personality has the ability to see the "big picture," and thus may have beneficial input for a local body and its ministry direction.

An apostolic personality may not have a deep appreciation for the "nuts and bolts" of daily operation. Stability is not his first priority and his frequent movement may be upsetting to some one gifted as a shepherd.

2. PROPHETIC - A prophetic personality tends to see things in black and white; there is not much gray area. While this person may be set in his opinion, the views expressed may sound indefinite and unrefined. A prophet needs help in the application of what he is sensing.

The behavior of a prophetic personality may seem peculiar and flighty. Because prophets are intractable and incomprehensible to many, they are regularly rejected and withdraw. It is painful - yet a prophet reappears because he feels compelled to keep speaking what he perceives. "Now you see him, now you don't" describes a common prophetic ministry pattern.

3. EVANGELICAL - Here is the salesman of the group. Gifted with communication, the evangelical personality is able to connect with others easily. He possesses persuasive

interpersonal skills. The evangelist receives a huge rush from "closing the sale" of the gospel. As one Christian salesman friend told me, "Conversion is like nose candy to an evangelist."

The evangelist becomes bored easily. Ordinary, daily discipleship may not be his strength. The evangelist tends to "blow in, blow up and blow out." While an evangelist may seem popular, he does not necessarily have deep, lasting personal relationships. Long term commitment is harder for him than for a shepherd or a teacher. An evangelist needs help discipling and training new converts.

4. SHEPHERD - A shepherd is often merciful and kind. He is concerned with everyday life and the continuous well-being of his "flock." Stable and reassuring, the shepherd wants his disciples to feel protected, fed, and loved. Sympathetic, the shepherd feels the pain of his flock. By nature of his function, he is an encourager - a trait that is very beneficial, but it should not be mistaken for a teaching gift.

A shepherd tends to be territorial, protective and - well – mundane. He is not necessarily interested in new ideas that "rock the boat." In fact, he may not even really be interested in body growth. A shepherd struggles with training and releasing members of his flock into outside ministry because it conflicts with his personal instinct for stability for the body. The shepherd needs help from the apostolic and teaching gifts to equip and release disciples.

5. TEACHER - A good teacher often has a heart for younger disciples. He discerns budding gifts and potential leadership and wants to develop them. A good teacher is an organized builder. He can assemble information and present it in a gradual sequence that cultivates step by step growth. The teacher does not fear failure by a disciple and shows grace eagerly.

Because he thinks organizationally, a teacher has to be careful not to lock into "systems" or "models." He needs input from the shepherd and prophetic in order not to lose sight of the organic, nor to repeat the same formulas in the same situation every time. If a "teacher" only preaches to large groups of people, and does not have a small group of persons that he personally trains, equips, and releases, he actually may not be a teacher, but an evangelist or an encourager.

Each of the five gifts has wonderful benefits. Each gift, however, has traits that may cause conflict with other gifts. The human tendency is to surround ourselves with people that see things the same way that we do. Unfortunately, this tendency means that ministry teams or church boards often have persons with the same gift on them. They are monolithic. Then, those ministries or committees wonder why they don't see healthy body growth or "can't seem to get anything done."

Interaction between persons with different gifts is challenging. Disparate gifts bring different and sometimes opposite perspectives to a situation. The views on a matter may be as diverse as the gifts considering it. But interaction over time with other gifts helps us grow. We learn the perspective and function of the other gifts, and begin to apply them in our own lives and ministry. When we work with other gifts, we begin to learn how to function in those other gifts.

PRINCIPLE: Cooperative fivefold function helps us to grow in other gifts.

So what is the key to transcending personal dysfunctions and the conflicting traits inherent in the gifts? If you have a close enough relationship to a person, you can work with them. If you perceive the love of God that dwells in a person's heart, you can overlook personality differences that would otherwise separate you. Relationship and love overcome immaturity.

PRINCIPLE: The depth of gift resource is equal to the depth of relationship.

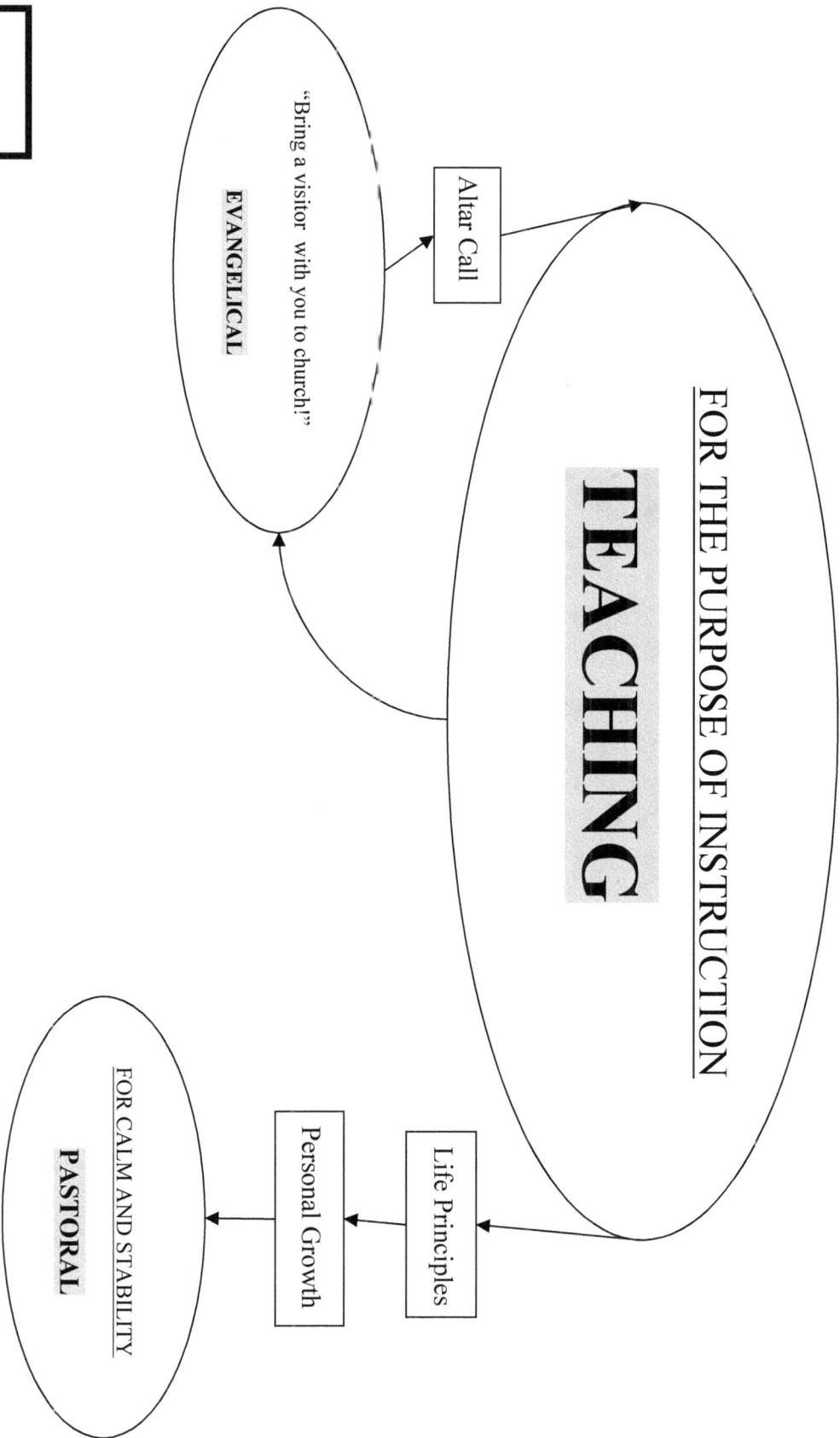

GUIDANCE

PROPHETIC

EVANGELICAL

"Bring a visitor with you to church!"

Altar Call

FOR THE PURPOSE OF INSTRUCTION

TEACHING

Life Principles

Personal Growth

PASTORAL

FOR CALM AND STABILITY

MEDITATION: "What then is Apollos? And what is Paul? Servants through whom you believed, even as the Lord gave opportunity. I planted, Apollos watered, but God was causing the growth. So then neither the one who plants nor the one who waters is anything, but God who causes the growth. Now he who plants and he who waters are one; but each will receive his own reward according to his own labor. For we are God's fellow-workers; you are God's field, God's building." I Cor. 3:5-9.

1. "I planted, Apollos watered." What gifts are described here?

2. Why are the one who plants and the one who waters not "anything?"

3. In what ways are the one who plants and the one who waters "one?"

4. What does it mean to be a "fellow-worker?"

5. Why are the fellow believers that repulse us the worst often the ones that we need the most?

REVIEW:
1. The church at Antioch demonstrated effective fivefold function.
2. Cooperative ministry yields resource.
3. By grace, God gives fantastic gifts to imperfect people.
4. Grace is necessary both in the giving and the receiving of the gift.
5. Cooperative fivefold function helps us grow in other gifts.
6. The depth of gift resource is equal to the depth of relationship.

LESSON 13 - HOPE

An advantage of reaching into the international community using the game of soccer is that I often had a large number of young men who wanted to play on the soccer team. Tryouts usually meant that I had a vast pool from which to choose players.

The negative aspect of this dynamic was that, at the end of tryouts, not all of the young men could make the team. I hated to cut players. Cutting a player felt like a breach of relationship. Both the players and I experienced pain in the process.

When I cut players, I told them they did not get a uniform. However, I offered to allow them to continue to practice with the team. In fact, if an injury occurred, they might even get the chance to suit up. Reactions of players varied when they received the dreaded news.

Abu had a "hair-trigger" temper. When I cut Abu, he cursed me up one side and down the other. I was a terrible coach. I failed to see that Abu was a superior player. It was obviously my fault. Furthermore, Abu didn't want to play on my team any way. Abu used some descriptive words for me and for the team that I coached. He then angrily stomped off. (He also returned to tryouts the following season. He made the team, and played on the team for a number of years.)

Kennedy was hurt by the cut. He thought a little bit, though, and said, "Coach, I just want to play soccer. I am going to come to practice, because I am going to get better. You just watch me." Kennedy faithfully came to practices that season and rode in the van to our games. Kennedy became like the team mascot. The guys loved to watch him dance. I told him he was the team manager. Sure enough, late in the season, we had some injuries. Kennedy was able to play in a few games. In one game, we had a substantial lead and I put Kennedy into the game. The players on the field began trying to set up plays for Kennedy to score. You should have seen the guys on the bench cheering for him to get a goal.

Boll was another player that I cut. Boll lacked speed and I didn't see where he could fit on the team. When I cut him, though, Boll decided to practice with the team. Boll functioned with quiet determination, and he took being "cut" in stride, although he assured me my judgement was wrong. By the middle of the season, it became obvious that I indeed

had made a mistake. Boll improved immensely that year. He not only played that season, but he became a valuable starter playing defense in the middle of the field. I was amazed at the potential that I apparently had missed.

I struggled with cutting players. I struggled relationally because I cared for all my players. The breach of relationship grieved me.

My biggest struggle, though, with cutting players from my team concerned what it communicated to them. Each player had potential. Cutting a player imposed a limitation on him. It said "There is only so far that you can go. You can't play at this level." Cutting a player could lead to a loss of hope.

I was the coach of the team. My decisions were based on what I thought was best for the team. I was only one person, though. My gifts were limited, and thus my perceptions were limited. As a result, each player was limited by my judgement, by my discernment, and by my vision. My own personal limitations were imposed on every player.

Anytime the decision making process boils down to one person, a limitation is imposed. The group of people impacted by those decisions is subjected to the gift limitations of that person. A decision maker who is primarily a shepherd might not discern apostolic or teaching potential. People gifted in those areas might lose hope because their potential is not recognized nor encouraged. They might abandon their call.

PRINCIPLE: Limitations in leadership lead to loss of hope.

Personally, I was pleased when a player showed the character to prove me wrong - to demonstrate ability beyond what I saw. It meant that the player did not lose hope.

PRESERVING HOPE

God told you that you will be king. God's prophet anointed you as king, and clearly

proclaimed that you are the rightful king. God confirmed that anointing with a mighty presence of His Holy Spirit.

Next, you become a national hero. Miraculously, you slay the mighty giant, Goliath, saving your king and your nation. Surely, it won't be long until you become king! But there is no way to anticipate what happened to you next.

The king you saved tries to kill you! You become a fugitive. For years, the king hunts you like a dog. You live like a refugee. The heat gets so hot that you cross battle lines, and fight in the service of your former enemies, the Philistines.

Then the Philistines decide they can't trust you. What do you do when you have been rejected by your own people and their enemies - the Israelites and the Philistines? Neither side wants you to fight for them, much less rule over them. They send you home.

But it gets worse! When you and the remaining people loyal to you return to your home base at Ziklag, you find that it has been sacked - burned with fire. Amalekites have raided it. They have plundered and burned the city. All of your possessions are gone. Your wives and children have been kidnapped. Your men are beside themselves. They lift up a huge lament. You and the people with you weep "until there was no strength left" to weep. Then, your own men talk about stoning you, "for all the people were embittered, each one because of his sons and his daughters." I Sam. 30:4-6.

Loss of hope is an awful thing. When we reach the bottom - the point where we weep until there is no strength left to weep, what can sustain us? What is there to give us hope?

David had a call from God. This call came in the form of an anointing as king. But David's leader, King Saul, did not submit to David's call. In fact, Saul did everything he could to discourage and stop David's call. He tried to kill him.

Now, at Ziklag, David is in a very difficult place. This crisis for David was the worst he ever faced. Personally, David lost everything. When he was a fugitive before, his men had always stood with him. But now, even his own men opposed him. What did David have to give him hope?

1. David could have given up. But David knew that God had anointed him and called him for a

purpose. He had an apostolic outlook. He knew he had a call from the Lord.

2. David could have saved his own skin. He could have fled and abandoned his own men. And justly so - weren't they plotting to stone him? But David had the heart of a shepherd. He was not going to abandon the people God had entrusted to his care.

3. David had knowledge of the Lord. When I read the Psalms of David, I see so many wonderful descriptions of the Lord and His Nature. How did David know so much about the Lord?

In Eph. 4:13, Paul says the five gifts help us attain "the unity of the faith and the knowledge of the Son of God." David's knowledge of God is evidence of his function in the five gifts, particularly the prophetic. In this moment of great distress, David refused to be embittered like his men. Instead, David drew upon his relationship with the Almighty. "But David strengthened himself in the Lord." I Sam. 30:6. When we exercise faith, we still have a basis for hope.

David utilized the prophetic gift. He didn't react in his own strength. He said, "I have got to hear from God." In classic fivefold function, David drew upon a prophetic resource from another person.

> Then David said to Abiathar the priest, the son of Ahimelech "Please bring me the ephod." So Abiathar brought the ephod to David. And David inquired of the Lord, saying, "Shall I pursue this band? Shall I overtake them?" And He said to him, "Pursue, for you shall surely overtake them, and you shall rescue all." I Sam. 30:7-8.

This prophetic word gave David hope. In obedience, David pursued and overtook the Amalekites. He recovered every person and every possession from the Amalekites. I Sam. 30:19. He not only recovered every possession of his own, but he recovered spoil that the Amalekites had seized from other raids. I Sam. 30:16. David's function in God's gifts protected him from losing hope. It kept him from abandoning his call from the Lord.

PRINCIPLE: Fivefold function preserves hope in hopeless situations.

POTENTIAL

When all five gifts have input, potential through all five functions is discerned. Opportunity exists for full potential in each area to be realized, and for call to be fulfilled. Hope is not lost.

> PRINCIPLE: Through operation of all five gifts, personal potential is not limited.

"And He gave some as apostles, and some as prophets, and some as evangelists, and some as pastors and teachers, for the equipping of the saints for the work of service, to the building up of the body of Christ; until we all attain to the unity of the faith, and of the knowledge of the Son of God, to a **mature man**, to the measure of the stature which belongs to the fullness of Christ." Eph. 4:11-13.

VISION

Boyz Club grew by leaps and bounds. In the summertime especially, kids overwhelmed us. We not only had youth from the area in which the church rented its apartment, but other youth came from a complex located a couple of miles away called The Park.

I began to wonder if we needed to go to The Park and begin another work there. Thousands of persons from lower income families lived in that complex. It was a place of great need.

Goose had been working with us at Boyz Club for a couple of years. Goose had a apostolic gift. At lunch one day, Goose said, "I drove by The Park the other day. We already have a number of guys coming to Boyz Club from The Park. It has a lot of needs. I think that the Lord may be calling me to go work at The Park."

I thought about the implications of what Goose proposed. From a shepherding perspective, it was not a good idea. We always performed ministry in teams. If Goose went

to The Park, he needed another leader to go with him. Our Boyz Club ministry would lose at least two leaders.

Even worse, if Goose went to The Park, the young men from the Park would stop coming to Boyz Club. We would lose members, and Boyz Club would shrink. Losing leaders and losing members. It might be risky for Boyz Club. Goose's proposal had some drawbacks.

From other perspectives though, the proposal was positive. From an apostolic perspective, Goose and a coworker would be sent to a new area to initiate a new work. From an evangelical perspective, the gospel would be proclaimed at The Park. From a prophetic perspective, Goose was confirming a vision that the Lord had already laid on my heart.

"Goose," I said, "I think the Lord has been showing me the same thing. Let's discuss how we can begin ministry at The Park."

When our Boyz Club ministry leaders met a few weeks later, Goose and I proposed a ministry at The Park. "Some one needs to go with Goose," I said.

Moses raised his hand. "I'll go with him."

The ministry at The Park grew over the next few months. In fact, if the truth be told, Goose and Moses improved on a number of the things at The Park that we were doing at Boyz Club.

One year later, the ministry leaders were meeting again. I always liked to review where we stood. "What happened over the past year?" I asked.

Moses spoke up. "I'll tell you what happened over the past year. Over the past year, the Lord doubled our ministry."

Without vision, there is no hope. Pro. 29:18. Vision is an area that desperately needs fivefold function. If Goose and I had simply viewed the call to The Park only from a shepherding perspective, the now vibrant and thriving ministry at The Park would never have happened. We needed all five gifts to understand and implement the vision that the Lord wanted to fulfill.

Key gifts for vision are the apostolic and the prophetic. The apostolic establishes new works, and is thus not fearful of potentially adverse circumstances inherent in a new work. The prophetic has an understanding of future actions the Lord may be prompting at that time.

> PRINCIPLE: If one of the five gifts is missing, the other gifts are handicapped.

I sat in a meeting with the leadership of my church. Leadership was seeking outside input to enhance the ministry and life of the church. The church asked a noted church leader to visit, review the operations of the church, and then advise leadership.

"What about vision?" asked an elder. "How does your church formulate its vision?"

The leader responded. "I am the person who sets the vision for my church. I receive the vision and then I communicate it to my elders. We then fulfill that vision."

I cringed when I heard that leader share. Vision should always arise from all five gifts. Many times, vision in a body is limited to one person. That key person may or may not have multiple fivefold gifts. If vision is limited to one person, the growth and function of the body is restricted by the extent of that person's vision or gift(s). The body can only progress as far as that person can see.

"Churches tend to reflect the personality of the pastor." How many times have you heard that saying? It means that the pastor has set the vision for that body according to his gifts and strengths.

Unfortunately, the "monovision" body may only be operating in one or two of the five gifts. The cycle of growth is broken. And more likely than not, the pastor experiences frequent burn out and frustration.

When one or two gifts dominate a body or a ministry, maturity is stymied. It is actually a form of oppression. King Saul was primarily concerned about his kingdom, his legacy, and his control. His insecurity and narcissism caused severe oppression of David. The maturity of a body should not depend on the maturity of one person or of one gift. In that case, members are frustrated because they can not grow corporately beyond the maturity level of that one person. The other gifts are restricted.

When all five gifts are functioning, credence (and deference) is accorded each gift.

Decision making is based on all five gifts. As a result, the body benefits from all five gifts, not just one or two. It is essential for church leadership to include persons with all five gifts.

Consider the leadership description of the church at Antioch - a body with effective fivefold function. Scripture does not say "Now there was at Antioch, in the church that was there a Senior Pastor, Barnabas, who led the congregation." Scripture says "Now there were at Antioch, in the church that was there, prophets and teachers: Barnabas, and Simeon who was called Niger, and Lucius of Cyrene, and Manaen who had been brought up with Herod the tetrarch, and Saul." Acts 13:1. How interesting that scripture lists five leaders of the church rather than one! How amazing that these five men were directed by the Holy Spirit, developed the vision, and then released Barnabas and Paul into their call!

> PRINCIPLE: Mature vision arises from the unified perspective of all five gifts.

In my experience, much "vision" that I have heard expressed is "air vision." The "air vision" may be valid and even on target, but it is ethereal. It is a vision that is somewhere "up there," but does not have meaningful application. The person expressing the vision may not possess the ability to implement it - to "put wheels on it." He lacks the gifts necessary to do so. The "air vision" often goes unfulfilled.

Where "air vision" meets "the ground" is the place that the "rubber meets the road." Effective fivefold function provides this application. Contained in the five gifts are sufficient abilities to fulfill God's vision. The "air vision" is fulfilled only by enhancement and implementation of the vision by other gifts.

BEYOND

Paul encourages us. "And since we have gifts that differ according to the grace given to us, let each exercise them accordingly; if prophecy, according to the proportion of his faith..." Rom. 12:6. We should desire to grow in our gift(s) in fuller and fuller measure as our faith in Him grows.

> PRINCIPLE: God calls each person to mature in the gift(s) which God gave him.

Growth in personal gifts will either be encouraged or discouraged. Fivefold function searches for gifts and it recognizes them. It encourages gifts to grow. It leads to hope.

Realization of our full potential in Christ achieves maturity. As a body, unified function of the five gifts is necessary to develop a complete vision, and then to implement that vision. Effective fivefold function removes limitations. God designed the five gifts to maximize creative potential of the Body in Him. When the five gifts function properly, they remove boundaries imposed by our flesh and by our circumstances.

> PRINCIPLE: Fivefold function leads to maturity of the body.

David pursued and recovered all from the Amalekites. But David's story did not end there. While David was fighting the Amalekites, he was not aware of the results of another battle - a battle in which Saul and three of his sons died. The day after the battle, the Philistines found Saul's body and stripped him of his weapons. I Sam. 31:8-9. But some one else got there first.

A little while later, a messenger came running to David in Ziklag. The messenger told David of the death of Saul. Then he presented David with a gift. Three days after David lost everything he had, a stranger handed him the crown and bracelet of Saul - the emblems of kingship of Israel. II Sam. 1:10.

We don't know the name of the messenger. David asked who he was. But the messenger only gave his identity.

The messenger said "I am an Amalekite." II Sam. 1:8.

David functioned in the gifts that God gave to him. He obeyed, and the Lord ordained that the crown of Israel be personally delivered to David by his enemy.

MEDITATION: "Now to Him who is able to do exceedingly abundantly beyond all that we ask or think, according to the power that works within us..." Eph. 3:20.

1. Paul writes this verse immediately before he lays out his vision for the body of Christ in Ephesians 4. Why was Paul so hopeful?

2. What is the meant by "the power that works within us?"

3. Do you agree that vision for a body should arise from the perspective of all five gifts?

4. How do you develop vision in your church or in your ministry?

5. How can you change function in your area(s) of ministry to realize full potential in Christ?

REVIEW:
1. Limitations in leadership lead to loss of hope.
2. Fivefold function preserves hope in hopeless situations.
3. Through operation all five gifts, personal potential is not limited.
4. If one of the five gifts is missing, the other gifts are handicapped.
5. Mature vision arises from the unified perspective of all five gifts.
6. God calls each person to mature in the gift(s) which God gave him.
7. Fivefold function leads to maturity of the body.

LOSS OF HOPE: "WHAT IF I DON'T FEEL CALLED TO ANYTHING?"

Call is dependent upon the Lord, not upon us. "And no one takes the honor to himself, but receives it when he is called by God, even as Aaron was." Heb. 5:4. We need to be submitted to the Lord with regard to call in our lives. Here are a few thoughts if you are in a place that you do not sense direction or call from the Lord in your personal life:

1. Don't stop seeking the Lord. Keep seeking Him every day for his will in your life. Pray, study, meditate, and live a godly life. Exercise faith that God is preparing you for His purpose as you seek Him, even if that preparation is slower and finer than you desire.

2. Function to the extent of the revelation and knowledge that you have now. The revelation of every believer is limited. Often, that limitation is due to sin or dysfunction in the heart of the believer. But God in His grace not only forgives our limitations, but helps us grow in faith and sanctification. He increases our revelation over time in the same way that He develops our call. "The kingdom of heaven is like a mustard seed, which a man took and sowed in his field; and this is smaller than all other seeds; but when it is full grown, it is larger than the garden plants, and becomes a tree, so that the birds of the air come and nest in its branches." Mt. 13:31b-32.

3. Don't just seek large, long term call. Often God calls us to small things on a daily basis. Our faithfulness in these small areas is huge. Using the small tiles of obedience in our life, God builds a powerful wall. "He who is faithful in a very little thing is faithful also in much; and he who is unrighteous in a very little thing is unrighteous also in much." Lk. 16:10.

4. Review your life tapestry in detail – especially your spiritual history. God often plants a sense of our spiritual destiny in our hearts at a young age. How has God worked in your life up to now? In what pathways and directions has He taken you?

5. Discern your gifts and talents. Equipping from God is relevant to your work for Him. What has God established and built within you? Gifts and talents suitable for what service?

LESSON 14- FULLNESS

As a coach, I experienced the pleasure of watching players improve over the course of a season. I also saw many players grow throughout their high school careers. Evan was one such player. When Evan tried out for the team in his freshman year, it was apparent that Evan had not played much soccer. He didn't have much skill, and he didn't look beyond the area covered by his position in the field. Evan had long legs, though, and those legs made it difficult for another player to dribble past him. Another player with the ball made a move on Evan, certain that he was around him. Evan just stuck out one of those long legs, though, and flicked the ball away. Evan played right defender his first year.

As Evan grew in defensive skill, his position changed. By the middle of his second year, Evan moved to center defender. Evan became a rock in the middle of the defense. He stopped many attacks coming through the center of the field.

By his senior season, Evan had learned how to pass and how to look beyond the areas of the field around him. I asked him to play one of the most demanding positions - center midfielder. A center midfielder plays on the offensive and defensive sides of the field. When we were on defense, Evan used his gifts as a defender. When we were on offense, Evan used his developed gifts as a playmaker. The role Evan played depended on the situation at the moment - defending or attacking. Evan's versatility was a great resource for the team. He became a playmaker, distributing the ball to all areas of the field. Evan was a captain and one of the most valuable players on a very good team.

Evan grew in his gifts such that he could play multiple roles. Evan could still play right defender as he did during his freshman year, if it was needed. But Evan had developed many other facets of his game. By the time he graduated, Evan could play almost any position on the field.

As we walk on our journey with the Lord through the years, we realize His deep mercy and love in the manner that He deals with us. He accepts us and loves us where we are. He allows us to work with our present gifts and limitations, and He helps us to grow in those gifts. Along the way, He may give us more gifts. But it is a gradual progression.

As I think about Evan, it gives me pleasure to reflect on his development as a player. Evan came to us as a gangly, unskilled teenager. Evan not only grew in his skills in the position at which he initially played. Evan learned other positions on the field. By the end of his high school career, he was a complete soccer player.

"And He gave some as apostles, and some as prophets, and some as evangelists, and some as pastors and teachers, for the equipping of the saints for the work of service, to the building up of the body of Christ; until we all attain to the unity of the faith, and of the knowledge of the Son of God, to a mature man, to the measure of the stature which belongs to **the fullness of Christ**." Eph. 4:11-13.

We are working toward realization of the "fullness of Christ." What we understand is that Jesus was complete in each of the gifts described in Ephesians 4:11. The five gifts were fully manifested in Him. The five gifts are gifts of Jesus.

1. APOSTLE - Jesus was sent into the world. "For I have come down from heaven, not to do My own will, but the will of Him who *sent* Me." Jn. 6:38. Jesus was the ultimate apostle, sent by the Father. "Therefore, holy brethren, partakers of a heavenly calling, consider Jesus, the Apostle and High Priest of our confession." Heb. 3:1 Jesus experienced a complete change of paradigm that literally "broke" barriers - from heaven to earth; from the divine to the human; and from death to life. Phil. 2:5-11.

2. PROPHET - Jesus had full prophetic revelation. "The Lord your God will raise up for you a prophet like me from among you, from among your countrymen, you shall listen to Him." Deut. 18:15. Jesus walked in this revelation. "Truly, truly, I say to you, the Son can do nothing of Himself, unless it is something He sees the Father doing; for whatever the Father does, these things the Son also does in like manner. For the Father loves the Son, and shows Him all things that He Himself is doing; and greater works than these will He show Him, that you may marvel." Jn. 5:19-20.

3. EVANGELIST - Jesus proclaimed the good news. "From that time, Jesus began to preach and say 'Repent, for the kingdom of God is at hand.'" Mt. 4:17. He was an evangelist. "The Spirit of the Lord is upon me, because He anointed Me to preach the gospel to the poor..." Lk. 4:18.

4. PASTOR - Jesus is the Great Shepherd of the sheep. Heb. 13:20. "I am the good Shepherd." Jn. 10:11. He cared for the disciples that the Father had entrusted to Him. "While I was with them, I was keeping them in thy name which Thou has given me; and I guarded them..." Jn. 17:12.

5. TEACHER - Jesus was the Teacher. "But do not be called Rabbi; for One is your teacher, and you are all brothers." Mt. 23:8. He instructed and trained His disciples so they could grow and minister in His Name. "As Thou didst send Me into the world, I also have sent them into the world." Jn. 17:18.

PRINCIPLE: The fivefold gifts are five ministries of Jesus.

Any time that a disciple functions in one of the gifts given by God, that disciple follows the example of Christ. That disciple aspires to the maturity in that gift that embodies the fullness of Christ.

Even more, as a disciple grows in each gift, he grows in the "knowledge of the Son of God." The character of Jesus defines these five gifts. Development of these gifts increases our understanding of the Nature and Person of Jesus.

PERSONAL GOALS

Our goal is the fullness of Christ. What steps should we take to reach this fullness?

1. The first goal is to mature in your present gifts. Identify the gifts that God has given you now. Understanding and acknowledging your gifts helps you discern the call(s) that God has for you.

Then seek to grow in the knowledge and use of those gifts. If God has appointed a shepherding gift in your life, grow into Christlike shepherding. Learn from other shepherds.

2. The second goal is to participate personally in working operation of the five gifts - fivefold function. This function occurs corporately in cooperation with other believers. Hopefully, the fivefold function occurs within a body of believers or within a specific ministry to fulfill the Cycle of Discipleship (although it is possible for ministries that are strong in one gift to cooperate with other ministries strong in other gifts). Seek out gifts different than your gift, and submit to them mutually. Participate in ministry cooperatively with those other gifts. This cooperative ministry is necessary for you to fulfill your call in the Lord. Amazing things happen as a body pursues God's plan for it according to His design.

Furthermore, you will learn from the other gifts.

The statistic is seemingly dismal. The number of persons who make a new commitment to Christ at an evangelistic crusade that are active in a church or whose lives have changed significantly 1 year later is very low. Most estimates hover near 5% - one in twenty! So when the advance team for the Billy Graham Carolinas Crusade came to Charlotte, N.C. in 1996, they connected with local churches. They connected with local churches for prayer and involvement during the crusade. But the team also asked local churches for help after the crusade. The Billy Graham team knew that after a strong evangelical gift operated during the crusade, churches could offer pastoral care and nurture. The team provided contact information of persons who made a commitment to local churches for follow up. So the Billy Graham Evangelistic Association partnered with local churches in their ministry. They wanted discipleship to continue after the crusade!

3. Finally, as God gives the measure of grace, strive to function personally in all five gifts. Desiring spiritual gifts is scriptural. Paul urged the Corinthian church "Pursue love, yet desire earnestly spiritual gifts, but especially that you may prophesy." I Cor. 14:1. Jesus ministered in all five gifts. If you desire to imitate Him personally, desire to grow in all five gifts as well.

Many people believe that fivefold function implies five people - one person for each gift.

This cooperation is possible, but not required, for effective fivefold function. In fact, scripture describes many saints that functioned in multiple gifts on many occasions.

Philip had a primary evangelical gift. This gift was so strong that Philip was called "the evangelist" by his brethren. Acts 21:8. But Philip needed to operate in other gifts in order to evangelize.

In Acts 8:26, an angel of the Lord tells Philip "Arise and go south to the road that descends from Jerusalem to Gaza." Philip was sent by the Lord. He operated apostolically.

When Philip saw a chariot on the road, the Spirit said to Philip "Go up and join this chariot." Acts 8:29. How did Philip know what to do? He heard from the Lord. He operated prophetically.

Now, based upon the foundation of apostolic and prophetic function, Philip could use his evangelical gift. He joined the Ethiopian eunuch in his chariot and "preached Jesus unto him." Acts 8:35. The eunuch believed and Philip baptized him.

Philip needed more than one gift in order to fulfill God's calling for him.

PRINCIPLE: Fullness of Christ implies the mature function of all five gifts.

I believe that God intended for us to work in teams. Teams can function with maturity in many gifts to fulfill the Cycle of Discipleship. Fivefold function, however, can occur with five people, two people or even one person. Just as Evan grew in different positions on the soccer field to become a complete soccer player, we can develop multiple gifts in the kingdom. Evan, however, still needed teammates.

Sometimes, however, God sends a person, and other believers don't join in that call. If that person desires to make disciples, he needs to grow in all five gifts. He will be required to proclaim, to shepherd, and to teach and train on his own.

I am not an ordained pastor, and I do not yet have the gift of healing. I have visited a number of refugee friends in the hospital through the years. When I visit them, I look for the opportunity to pray with them and to ask the Lord for comfort and for healing. I am

164

not trying to be presumptuous. I am trying to fulfill the ministry of Jesus.

There are specific situations to which God calls us. Different gifts are needed in different situations. The gift needed at the moment may not be our primary gift. But if you are the person that God has placed in that situation, you may need to function in an unfamiliar role due to the urgency of the moment. If the ministry of Jesus is to be accomplished, we may need to operate in another gift.

> PRINCIPLE: A mature Christian operates in each gift depending on the present need and mission.

Here is a caution: Perhaps the most disastrous dynamic is for one person to go out and try to "solo" in all five gifts unnecessarily. This attempt is often based on a prideful belief that "I have the package." The gifts are not the goal. The Lord and His kingdom's work are the goal. That kingdom is a corporate entity, not an individual one. To the extent possible, submit to others and minister together with them. There is a reason that Jesus sent His disciples out to minister in pairs, and that the same disciples followed this model in the Book of Acts.

"WHERE TWO OR THREE HAVE GATHERED IN MY NAME"

On the night of August 21, 2006, I had a dream.

I was in a congregation of worshipers. In front of the congregation, there was a stage. On the stage was a worship band leading worship. A pastor and other leaders of the congregation were on the stage as well.

I then saw a young man there with curly red hair and a red beard in the congregation. He was not a leader in the congregation and he did not have a title or a position. When I saw him in my dream, though, I thought to myself, "He has the anointing."

Without invitation, the red-haired man stepped forward on the stage. He asked the worship band to stop playing and to step off the stage. The band came down from the stage to pack up their instruments. They left willingly without rancor or complaint. The pastor also stepped off the stage.

The redheaded man began singing and leading worship alone. He was not a very good singer. The congregation, however, followed suit as he led the meeting.

Then, the Holy Spirit fell. In the rows behind me on the right half of the congregation, it was as if a wave hit. Starting on the right side and moving across the congregation to the left side, people fell down under the power of the Holy Spirit. No one was praying for them individually. The red-haired man was just singing and praying from the stage.

The Holy Spirit moved in a visible, palpable, and powerful way across the congregation as it experienced a deep and heavy Presence.

This dream describes both the operation of the five gifts and effective fivefold function.

In order for the red-haired man to step forward without invitation, God had to call him for that moment. God had to tell him "Go and minister." The red-haired man was sent. He operated boldly and apostolically.

In order for the congregational leadership and worship band to discern that the red-haired man had an anointing, they had to operate prophetically. They had to determine whether or not God was working through the red-haired man.

When the leadership and congregation submitted to the call of the red-haired man, it demonstrated mature fivefold function. They deferred and willingly participated in his call. The worship band was more talented than he was. They were seeking the Lord, though, and not their own glory or status. They further obviously had a heart to encourage and train younger people in worship - a teaching perspective. Their submission led to true worship in the Spirit.

What was the impact of fivefold gifts and function by the congregation? My conclusion is that it invited and welcomed the Holy Spirit. It ushered in the Presence of the Lord.

PRINCIPLE: The fullness of Christ is Present in fivefold function.

MEDITATION: "For of His fullness we have all received, and grace upon grace." Jn. 1:16.

1. Who is "all" in this verse?

2. Describe the ways in which you have received of the "fullness of Christ?"

3. Do you agree with the three personal goals described in this chapter? (See #2, 4 and 5 below)

4. If so, how do the three personal goals apply to you?

REVIEW:

1. The fivefold gifts are five ministries of Jesus.

2. The first personal goal is to mature in your present gifts.

3. Understanding and acknowledging your gifts helps you discern the call(s) that God has for you.

4. The second personal goal is to participate in working operation of the five gifts - fivefold function.

5. The third personal goal, as God gives the measure of grace, is to function in all five gifts.

6. Fullness of Christ implies the mature function of all five gifts.

7. A mature Christian operates in each gift depending on the present need and mission.

8. The fullness of Christ is Present in fivefold function.

LESSON 15 - FOUNDATION

One Valentine's Day, my wife gave me a unique and wonderful Valentine's Day present. When I arrived home from work that day, I found a number of small Valentine's cards strategically placed in spots where I would find them. The cards said, "I love you because..." Each card had a different reason written on it by my wife - a different reason why she loved me.

As I found the cards, they had messages like "I love you because you are my beloved husband;" "I love you because you are fun to be with;" "I love you because you treasure your family;" and "I love you because you encourage me to grow."

The last card I found, though, gave me pause. It read "I love you because you love your refugee boys." I had to think about that one. It honestly surprised me. But my wife was right. I did - and still do have - a deep love for those refugee boys.

What lasts? As the world advances technologically, humans have become acclimated to the temporary entertainment hit. They expect immediate gratification - repeatable immediate gratification. So media broadcast the flashy sound byte. The internet feeds the short attention span image. Movies are simply compilations of ridiculous action sequences - each scene contrived to surpass the previous sensation. When it is over, we already crave the next hit. Like any addiction, it is thrilling, yet so unfulfilling.

All around us, people search for something that remains - a feeling...or an idea...a motivation...or a ministry. What is permanent? Before Paul describes the keys to equipping, building, maturity, and fullness in Ephesians 4, he lays a foundation in Ephesians 3.

MOTIVATION AND ENDURANCE

One summer our church held a Vacation Bible School at the inner city apartment complex at which I regularly ministered. Instead of holding the Vacation Bible School for one week, the church held sessions each Sunday evening for five weeks. On each Sunday an army of volunteers came from the church to the apartments - serving food, organizing games, and teaching classes on the green in the middle of the complex. We encouraged the volunteers to get to know the apartment residents and to try to develop relationships with them. Many church members bravely stretched their "comfort zones" to meet refugee families and to spend time with them during the event.

The Vacation Bible School ended. The next week on Sunday evening, I was out there at the apartments alone, just as I had done regularly for quite a while. One of the children came up to me. He looked around puzzled and asked, "Where is everybody?"

"Vacation Bible School is over and they went home," I replied.

"Oh!" the child said. He had a disappointed expression.

I tried to think of something to temper the obvious disappointment. "I'm here" I said.

The child gave me a look that said "So what. You're old hat." He slowly shook his head, and walked away.

Please understand, I was thankful for the large number of volunteers that came and sacrificed their time to teach, play and interact with the refugee families during that Vacation Bible School. But if genuine care existed - a deep, Godly love - the relationships would have continued. When you care for somebody, you do not abandon him.

1. You can not be motivated by duty. If duty is your chief motive, you will do just enough to assuage your guilt...just enough to say you have done your rightful duty, and then quit. You will throw a proverbial bone to the people, but in the final analysis, they will still be a dog.

What is worse, they will know it. Jesus rebuked the Pharisees for this type of "ministry." "But woe to you Pharisees! For you pay tithe of mint and rue and every kind of garden herb, and yet disregard justice and the love of God; but these are the things you should have done without neglecting the others." Lk. 11:42.

2. You can not be motivated by the idea of your ministry. If "success" of your ministry is your motivation, you will do what it takes to make your ministry "successful" in your own eyes. You will disdain actual care for other people. A fundamental part of serving people is discerning their

felt needs - discovering their needs as they see them, not just as you see them. People discern your motivation. They know whether what you are doing is motivated by your own selfish needs, or by a Godly love and a Godly concern for them and for their needs.

3. You can not be motivated by making yourself feel good. If gratification is your motivation, you will minister until you are satisfied, and then stop.

We often help people so they will tell us "Thank you." It makes us feel like benefactors - that other people are beholden to us. Gratitude is a form of adulation. Gratitude imparts a feeling of power to its recipient.

Paul was a farmer in the mountains. Tall and lanky, he possessed a deep voice and leathery skin hardened by years of work under the hot sun. Paul was a godly man raised by godly parents. He was a "salt of the earth" type - a humble man of the soil.

Paul read in scripture that God instructed the Israelites not to harvest the corners of their field in order to allow the poor and hungry to glean them to have something to eat. Lev. 23:22. For years, Paul planted full fields of corn. However, he did not harvest the outer rows to allow any needy person to come and pick the corn to eat.

People of Paul's community knew of Paul's generosity. But some people take advantage of generosity. One day a merchant from the local Farmer's Market drove his truck to the field farthest from the farm house, and begin picking Paul's corn and putting it in the back of his pickup. He intended to take the corn to the Farmer's Market and sell it there.

As the merchant was hurriedly picking ears of corn, over the crest of the hill came Paul riding his farm tractor. Paul was an imposing figure when he stood on the ground. Paul was big, strong man. At the top of the hill sitting on his tractor, Paul must have looked like a giant. The merchant scrambled to try to cover the corn in the back of the pickup as Paul rode up to him.

Paul stopped at the pickup. Cowering, the merchant looked up at the raw-boned farmer, not sure what to expect. He was caught red handed. Paul looked at the merchant and then slowly shook his head. "Well," Paul said in his deep, booming voice, "you better

get some before it all gets gone."

Relieved, the merchant jumped in his pickup and sped away as fast as he could.

Paul's motivation in sharing his corn was to share God's love. If Paul had left the corn in his fields for adulation or gratitude, he would have been enraged that the merchant was abusing his charity. Instead, Paul left the evil doer to God's hand.

4. If love is the motivation of your call, you will work until God's love - the love that yourself experience - is shed abroad in their hearts. Effective ministry begins with the love of Christ. In order for you to help transform others, you yourself must first be transformed. You must be "rooted and grounded in love." Eph. 3:17. As Oswald Chambers says in My Utmost for His Highest (January 17), "God gets me into a relationship with Himself whereby I understand His call, then I do things out of sheer love for Him on my own account. To serve God is the deliberate love-gift of a nature that has heard the call of God."

If you have experienced the love of Christ, then you will want to share that love with others. You will say, "I have experienced this deep, loving and abiding Presence. I want you to have that same Presence." Like the apostle Paul, the desire from the very core of your being will be that each person will "know the breadth and length and height and depth" of the love of Christ. Eph. 3:18.

A minister motivated by God's love will keep coming back to relate to, and to care for, the people that are the object of that love. If you love them, you will seek a relationship with them. You will seek them out and not abandon them. If you love them with God's love, you will maintain regular contact with them, and try to go deeper, and deeper, and deeper still.

A ministry motivated by God's love lasts. Sometimes, it lasts a lifetime - or longer.

> PRINCIPLE: A program is finite. A relationship can last forever.

A LESSON IN FOUNDATION

Paul poured his heart and soul into the Ephesian church. In Acts 19, we read that Paul spent years in Ephesus - preaching, teaching, admonishing, and loving. In fact, the word "Ephesus" means "desirable." (Reference: *International Standard Bible Encyclopedia*)

In Acts 20, Paul calls the elders of Ephesus to him, and delivers to them a moving encouragement and instruction. Acts 20:18-35. Then, in one of the most poignant scenes in scripture, Paul and the elders at Ephesus embrace and weep.

> And when [Paul] had said these things, he knelt down and prayed with them all. And they began to weep aloud and embraced Paul, and repeatedly kissed him, grieving especially over the word which he had spoken, that they should see his face no more. And they were accompanying him to the ship. Acts 20:36-38.

Later in his life, Paul wrote the epistle to "the saints who are at Ephesus, and who are faithful in Christ Jesus." Eph. 1:1. At one point, he sent Tychicus to minister to the Ephesians. II Tim. 4:12. What a wonderful heritage possessed by the church at Ephesus!

You may have sensed a strong undercurrent in the last few chapters of this book. Those chapters discussed aspects of fivefold function. But they also described some of the attitudes necessary for that function.

Consider Barnabas who was full of encouragement for the saints. Barnabas had an attitude of service toward younger men like Saul and Mark who were "under" him. He equipped them to attain great heights in the kingdom of God.

Consider David whose love and fear of God kept him from presumption. David's attitude of submission was remarkable, and his God-conscious heart led him into new depths of worship.

Consider Philip whose attitude of sensitivity to the leading of the Holy Spirit prompted him to boldness in preaching and to freedom of movement.

These men occupied important offices or functions. Yet their ministry flowed from hearts that were tender toward God and toward others. Our motivation determines our effectiveness. And our motivation arises from our desires and attitudes.

Take time to consider attitudes necessary to fulfill the call of God – attitudes like humility, gentleness, patience, service and care. Eph. 4:1-3. Search your own heart and the impact of Christ on it. Discern the meaning of the imitation of Jesus on your life. Changes in your attitudes through your deep devotional life will enhance your fivefold function.

Paul emphasized attitude of the heart in his letter to the Ephesian church. He knew that a heart for ministry fundamentally arises from a heart of love.

For this reason, I bow my knees before the Father, from whom every family in heaven and on earth derives its name, that He would grant you, according to the riches of His glory, to be strengthened with power through His Spirit in the inner man; so that Christ may dwell in your hearts through faith; and that you, being rooted and grounded in love, may be able to comprehend with all the saints what is the breadth and length and height and depth, and to know the love of Christ which surpasses knowledge, that you may be filled up **to all the fullness of God**. Eph. 3:14-19.

Paul wanted the Ephesian church to experience all the fullness of God. As he began to explain fivefold function, he made it clear that effective function arose from a heart of love.

The final Biblical message directed to the Ephesian church is found in Revelation.

I know your deeds and your toil and perseverance, and that you cannot endure evil men, and you put to the test those who call themselves apostles, and they are not, and you found them to be false; and you have perseverance and have endured for My name's sake, and have not grown weary. But I have this against you, **that you have left your first love.** Remember therefore from where you have fallen, and repent and do the deeds you did at first; or else I am coming to you, and will remove your lampstand out of its place - unless you repent. Rev. 2:2-5.

What happened to the Ephesian church? Those beloved saints - the ones that Paul urged to the fullness of Christ - endured. They functioned well in good deeds, toil, perseverance, and corporate integrity. But they did not remain rooted and grounded in God's love. They forsook the breadth and length and height and depth. Their motivation was not pure.

Today, the Ephesian church is no more. Ephesus no longer exists. The city whose name means "desirable" now lies desolate.

PRINCIPLE: Effective fivefold operation occurs as a result of
Godly attitudes as much as a result of function, roles or process.

MEDITATION: "All the ways of a man are clean in his own sight, But the Lord weighs the motives." Pro. 16:2.

1. Identify three personal attitudes that you believe imitate Jesus.

2. Identify three attitudes toward others that you believe imitate Jesus.

3. What is the state of your heart with regard to these attitudes?

4. What attitudes do you display in the ministry that you now perform?

5. Is there any selfishness in your motivation for your ministry?

REVIEW:

1. As we participate in ministry, it is important to discern our motivation.

2. If duty is your chief motive, you will do just enough to assuage your guilt, and then quit.

3. If "success" of your ministry is your motivation, you will do what it takes to make your ministry "successful" in your own eyes.

4. If gratification is your motivation, you will minister until you are satisfied, and then stop.

5. Effective ministry begins with the love of Christ.

6. In order for you to help transform others, you yourself must first be transformed.

7. If you have experienced the love of Christ, then you will want to share that love with others.

8. A program is finite. A relationship can last forever.

9. Effective fivefold operation is a result of Godly attitudes as much as a result of function, roles or process.

POSTLOGUE – A CAUTION

"And He gave some as apostles, and some as prophets, and some as evangelists, and some as pastors and teachers, for the equipping of the saints for the work of service, to the building up of the body of Christ; until we all attain to the unity of the faith, and of the knowledge of the Son of God, to a mature man, to the measure of the stature which belongs to the fullness of Christ." Eph. 4:11-13.

A number of years ago, five men came together in a room in Charlotte, North Carolina. The five men were leading Christians in the city. Three of the five men were senior pastors of prominent churches in the city.

The five men came together for a reason. Each man had a distinct gift. One was apostolic. Another was prophetic. Yet another was an evangelist. The fourth was a pastor. And the fifth was a noted teacher. The five men came together because of Ephesians 4. They properly discerned that the five gifts in Ephesians 4:11 had a purpose. They understood that the five gifts were intended to work together. The plan was for the five gifts to come together. Each man would take his rightful position. Then they would see what God would do.

So the five men came together. They prayed. They talked. They sought. And what happened as a result was...

Well, what happened was nothing. Nothing of note came out of that gathering of five men.

My concern is that persons who try to implement fivefold ministry will copy these five men. These men were all wonderful men of God, but they acted according to their understanding. They thought that each gift was vested in an individual – creating five offices, as it were. If those five officials just came together, effective fivefold function would result.

But it didn't. Something was missing. What the five men lacked was a call from God through which they could apply their gifts. The meeting focused on the gifts themselves rather than on the purpose of the gifts.

Here is a caution: Don't initially identify your gift, and then try to ascend to a position involving that gift. This book begins with the idea of call, rather than with a description of the gifts themselves, for a reason. The gifts only have meaning if they are used for God's intended purpose.

So instead of focusing on gift or position, first seek God for His call for your life. Where is He calling you to go? What is He calling you to do? Understand that call may occur immediately, or it may take many years. Don't be frustrated if you don't instantly see the call that God has on your life. It is God's timing. He weaves events and revelation into our life in a fantastic way. It is a tapestry. In fact, His call may be completely different than the position that you are now in. Continue to seek Him fervently on a daily basis.

Then when the call of God does come, use the gifts that God has given to fulfill that call so God may be glorified. Remember that the five gifts are not the goal. The five gifts are tools given to help reach the goal – maturity of the Body of Christ in Him. The gifts are given according to the measure of His grace in order to fulfill His will. May you grow in these gifts as they are needed to fulfill His call.

And as you exercise those gifts, don't forget the Cycle of Discipleship! Discipleship is the essence of Jesus' final instructions to His disciples. It is my prayer that you realize how you fit into this cycle in deeper and deeper measure to maturity.

Finally, remember that kingdom potential is not just individual. It is corporate. Each body of believers has huge potential within God's kingdom. God calls a group or a body of believers to a work. On an individual level, the kingdom potential is a multiple. For a committed group, the kingdom potential is exponential. When Paul wrote his vision for the body of Christ in Ephesians 4, he understood that it was something much bigger than himself. It was a sum much larger than the individual parts. Eph. 4:16.

Paul had incredible vision when he wrote the Book of Ephesians. It was a vision based on revelation from God, and a vision based on profound experience from the call that God issued to him. It was a vision that arose from operating in the gifts that God gave to Paul.

It was a vision of the fullness of Christ.

For most of my life, when I read scripture, I read it in terms of myself – an individual. I wanted to know it, to incorporate it, and to apply it to my personal walk and ministry.

A number of years ago, though, I began to read scripture from a corporate perspective – the perspective of one part of a larger body. I asked the Lord not only what the scripture meant for myself, but also what the scripture meant for Christ's body – the "fullness of Him who fills all in all." Eph. 1:23. In the next book, we will explore call from a corporate perspective, with the hope that we can fulfill our destiny in Him as His body...His beloved...the fullness of Christ.

"Now to Him who is able to do exceeding abundantly beyond all that we ask or think, according to the power that works within us, to Him be the glory in the church and in Christ Jesus to all generations forever and ever. Amen." Eph. 3:20-21.

NOTES:

NOTES:

NOTES:

NOTES:

NOTES: